OVERCOMING FAILURE

Strategies for Bouncing Back from Setbacks and Learning from Mistakes

Charlie Moore

Table of Contents

Chapter 1: Embracing Failure as a Catalyst for Growth

How failure can serve as a powerful tool for personal and professional development: Failure can be a powerful tool for personal and professional development in several ways:

1. Learning from Mistakes: Failure provides an opportunity for reflection and self-assessment. When we experience failure, we can analyze what went wrong, identify the mistakes we made, and learn from them. This process of self-reflection allows us to gain insights into our strengths and weaknesses and helps us make better-informed decisions in the future.

2. Building Resilience: Failure can toughen us mentally and emotionally. It challenges us to bounce back from setbacks, faces adversity, and persevere despite disappointment and setbacks. Each time we overcome failure, we become more resilient, developing the mental and emotional toughness needed to navigate challenges and setbacks in the future.

3. Developing Problem-Solving Skills: Failure often presents us with problems to solve. When we encounter failure, we are forced to think critically, analyze the situation, and come up with creative solutions to address the issues at hand. This cultivates our problem-solving skills, helping us become better equipped to handle complex situations and find innovative ways to overcome obstacles.

4. Building Character and Strength: Failure can be a humbling experience that tests our character and inner strength. It can reveal our true values, beliefs, and convictions, and profoundly shape our character. It can also help us develop perseverance, empathy, and humility, which are essential for personal and professional growth.

5. Fostering Innovation and Creativity: Failure can spark innovation and creativity. When our initial attempts fail, we are often forced to think outside the box, explore new ideas, and experiment with different approaches. This fosters a culture of innovation and creativity, encouraging us to explore new possibilities and come up with fresh solutions to problems.

6. Building Self-Awareness: Failure can lead to increased self-awareness. When we experience failure, we are forced to confront our limitations, weaknesses, and areas for improvement. This self-awareness allows us to reflect on our thoughts, behaviors, and actions, and make necessary adjustments to enhance our performance and personal growth.

7. Encouraging Risk-Taking and Growth Mindset: Failure can encourage us to take calculated risks and step out of our comfort zones. It pushes us to embrace a growth mindset, where we see failure as an opportunity to learn, grow, and improve, rather than a reflection of our self-worth. This mindset encourages continuous learning, innovation, and the pursuit of excellence.

8. Building Resilient Networks and Support Systems: Failure can also strengthen our networks and support systems. It can help us realize the importance of having a strong support system in our personal and professional lives. When we face failure, the support of friends, mentors, and colleagues can provide encouragement, guidance, and valuable perspectives that help us navigate through tough times.

Failure can serve as a powerful tool for personal and professional development. It provides opportunities for learning, resilience building, problem-solving, character development, innovation, and self-awareness. By embracing failure as a natural part of life's journey and learning from it, we can grow, develop new skills, and ultimately achieve greater success in our personal and professional lives.

What is the mindset shift needed to view failure as an opportunity for learning and growth?

A mindset shift is required to view failure as an opportunity for learning and growth. Here are some key mindset shifts that can help:

1. Embracing a Growth Mindset: Adopting a growth mindset involves seeing failure as a chance to learn and improve, rather than as a reflection of our abilities or self-worth. It's about believing that our intelligence, abilities, and skills can be developed through effort, learning, and perseverance. With a growth mindset, we see failure as a stepping stone toward growth and development, and we are more likely

to persevere, learn from our mistakes, and try again with a new approach.

2. Reframing Failure as Feedback: Instead of seeing failure as a negative outcome, we can reframe it as feedback. Failure provides valuable information about what didn't work, what can be improved, and what can be done differently next time. By reframing failure as feedback, we can approach it with curiosity, openness, and a willingness to learn from the experience.

3. Shifting from Blame to Responsibility: Instead of blaming ourselves or others for failure, we can take responsibility for our actions and outcomes. This involves acknowledging our role in the failure, identifying what we could have done differently, and taking ownership of our mistakes. By taking responsibility, we can focus on learning from our failures and making constructive changes moving forward.

4. Cultivating a Positive Mindset: Viewing failure as an opportunity for learning and growth requires cultivating a positive mindset. This involves shifting our focus from dwelling on the negative aspects of failure to recognizing the potential for growth and improvement. It's about looking for the silver lining, finding the lessons learned, and maintaining an optimistic outlook despite setbacks.

5. Emphasizing Process over Outcome: Instead of focusing solely on the outcome, we can focus on the process. This means valuing the effort, learning, and progress made, regardless of the outcome. By emphasizing the process, we can see failure as a necessary part of the journey toward success, and appreciate the learning and growth that can occur along the way.

6. Embracing a "Fail Forward" Mentality: Rather than fearing failure, we can embrace a "fail forward" mentality, where we see failure as a stepping stone towards progress. This involves reframing failure as a natural part of the learning process, and recognizing that failure can provide valuable insights, experiences, and opportunities for growth.

7. Practicing Self-Compassion: When we experience failure, it's important to practice self-compassion. This means being kind and

understanding towards ourselves, and not being too harsh or critical. It involves recognizing that failure is a part of being human and treating ourselves with the same kindness, empathy, and understanding that we would offer to others.

Shifting our mindset to view failure as an opportunity for learning and growth involves adopting a growth mindset, reframing failure as feedback, taking responsibility, cultivating a positive mindset, emphasizing the process, embracing a "fail forward" mentality, and practicing self-compassion. By adopting these mindset shifts, we can transform our relationship with failure and leverage it as a powerful personal and professional development tool.

Overcoming the fear of failure that often holds us back from taking risks and pursuing our goals.

The fear of failure can often hold us back from taking risks and pursuing our goals. However, there are several strategies that can help us overcome this fear and move forward toward our aspirations:

1. Identify and Challenge Negative Beliefs: Often, fear of failure is fueled by negative beliefs we hold about ourselves or the consequences of failure. Identifying and challenging these beliefs can help us gain perspective and realize that they may not be accurate or helpful. For example, we may have beliefs such as "Failure means I'm not good enough" or "Failure will ruin my reputation." By challenging these beliefs and replacing them with more empowering and realistic ones, we can reduce the fear of failure and gain confidence in taking risks.

2. Reframe Failure as an Opportunity: Instead of viewing failure as a purely negative outcome, we can reframe it as an opportunity for growth and learning. By seeing failure as a chance to gain valuable experience, learn from mistakes, and improve ourselves, we can shift our mindset and reduce the fear associated with it.

3. Set Realistic Expectations: Setting realistic expectations for ourselves and our goals can help reduce the fear of failure. Understanding that setbacks and failures are a normal part of any journey towards success can help us approach them with a more balanced and resilient mindset.

It's important to recognize that failure does not necessarily equate to total defeat, but rather as a stepping stone towards progress.

4. Break Goals into Smaller, Achievable Steps: Breaking our goals into smaller, achievable steps can make them feel more manageable and less intimidating. This approach allows us to focus on making progress one step at a time and reduces the pressure of potential failure. Celebrating each small success along the way can also help build momentum and motivation.

5. Cultivate a Supportive Network: Surrounding ourselves with a supportive network of friends, mentors, or colleagues can provide encouragement, motivation, and perspective when facing the fear of failure. Having people who believe in us, provide feedback, and offer support can help us build resilience and overcome the fear of failure.

6. Build Resilience and Coping Skills: Developing resilience and coping skills can help us navigate the challenges and setbacks that come with taking risks and facing failure. Techniques such as mindfulness, self-care, and stress management can help us build emotional strength and bounce back from failures with a more positive outlook.

7. Take Action and Face Your Fears: Taking action despite the fear of failure is a powerful way to overcome it. By confronting our fears and taking calculated risks, we can gradually desensitize ourselves to the fear of failure and build our confidence in facing challenges. Remember that taking action doesn't necessarily mean we won't fail, but it's a step toward growth and progress.

8. Learn from Past Failures: Reflecting on past failures and extracting lessons from them can be a valuable learning process. By identifying what went wrong, what we could have done differently, and what we learned, we can turn failures into opportunities for improvement and growth. This helps us develop a more positive and proactive mindset toward failure.

Overcoming the fear of failure requires a combination of challenging negative beliefs, reframing failure as an opportunity, setting realistic expectations, breaking goals into smaller steps, cultivating a supportive network, building resilience and coping skills, taking action, and learning from past failures. By adopting these strategies, we can overcome the fear of failure and take meaningful steps towards pursuing our goals and realizing our aspirations.

Chapter 2: Analyzing the Root Causes of Failure

What are the various root causes of failure?

Failure can have various root causes, and it's important to understand these causes in order to effectively address and overcome them. Some common root causes of failure include:

1. Lack of Planning and Preparation: Failure can occur when there is insufficient planning or preparation before embarking on a task or project. Without a clear roadmap, goals, and adequate resources, the chances of failure increase.

2. Inadequate Skills or Knowledge: Lack of necessary skills or knowledge can be a root cause of failure. If we do not possess the required expertise or qualifications for a task or project, it can lead to subpar performance and eventual failure.

3. Poor Decision-making: Making poor decisions, such as hasty or uninformed choices, can lead to failure. Decision-making involves critical thinking, weighing pros and cons, considering alternatives, and making informed choices. Poor decision-making can result in wrong directions, missed opportunities, or costly mistakes.

4. Fear of Taking Risks: Fear of taking risks and stepping out of one's comfort zone can hinder progress and lead to failure. Taking calculated risks is often necessary for growth and success, and being overly cautious or risk-averse can prevent one from seizing opportunities.

5. Lack of Persistence and Resilience: Giving up too soon or lacking persistence in the face of challenges can lead to failure. Success often requires perseverance, resilience, and the ability to bounce back from setbacks. Without these qualities, failure may be more likely.

6. Ineffective Communication and Collaboration: Poor communication and collaboration can lead to misunderstandings, misaligned expectations, and conflicts, which can ultimately result in failure. Effective communication and collaboration are crucial for achieving common goals and avoiding failures caused by miscommunication or lack of teamwork.

7. External Factors and Circumstances: External factors such as market conditions, economic changes, or unexpected events beyond our control can also lead to failure. Sometimes, despite careful planning and preparation, unforeseen circumstances can disrupt plans and result in failure.

8. Lack of Motivation and Focus: Lack of motivation, focus, or commitment towards goals can lead to failure. Maintaining a clear sense of purpose, setting priorities, and staying motivated are important factors in achieving success and avoiding failure.

9. Inadequate Resource Management: Poor management of resources, such as time, finances, or personnel, can also be a root cause of failure. Mismanagement of resources can result in inefficiencies, delays, and ultimately failure to achieve objectives.

10. Personal Limitations and Mindset: Personal limitations, such as self-doubt, negative mindset, or limiting beliefs, can also contribute to failure. Our mindset and beliefs shape our actions and outcomes, and a negative or self-limiting mindset can hinder success and lead to failure.

It's important to recognize that failure can have multiple root causes, and it's crucial to identify and address these causes in order to learn from failures, make improvements, and move towards success. Reflecting on the root causes of failure can provide valuable insights and guide us towards taking corrective actions to prevent future failures.

The strategies for identifying and addressing Lack of Planning and Preparation

When lack of planning and preparation is identified as a root cause of failure, it's important to take proactive steps to prevent it from recurring in the future. Here are some strategies to address the issue:

1. Establish a clear and detailed plan: Develop a comprehensive plan that outlines the objectives, goals, timelines, resources, and milestones of the task or project. Ensure that all team members are aware of the plan and aligned with the expectations. Regularly review and update the plan as needed.

2. Conduct thorough research and analysis: Gather all the relevant information and data necessary for the task or project. Conduct thorough research and analysis to identify potential challenges, risks, and opportunities. This will enable better decision-making and help in developing an effective plan.

3. Allocate adequate resources: Ensure that sufficient resources, such as time, budget, manpower, and tools, are allocated to the task or project. Identify any potential resource gaps and take necessary measures to address them. Adequate resource allocation is critical for successful planning and preparation.

4. Define roles and responsibilities: Clearly define roles and responsibilities of team members involved in the task or project. Ensure that everyone understands their roles and responsibilities and is accountable for their tasks. This will prevent confusion and ensure smooth execution of the plan.

5. Develop contingency plans: Anticipate potential risks and challenges and develop contingency plans to mitigate them. Identify alternative approaches or solutions in case of unexpected issues. Having contingency plans in place can help in addressing unforeseen situations and minimizing the impact of failures.

6. Foster open communication and collaboration: Encourage open communication and collaboration among team members. Foster a culture where team members feel comfortable sharing their ideas, concerns, and feedback. Regularly review progress and performance, and address any issues or gaps in planning and preparation through effective communication.

7. Learn from past failures: Reflect on past failures and identify the lessons learned. Use these insights to improve planning and preparation for future tasks or projects. Consider conducting post-mortem reviews to understand what went wrong and how to prevent similar failures in the future.

8. Invest in training and skill development: Ensure that team members have the necessary skills and knowledge to execute the plan

effectively. Invest in training and skill development programs to enhance the capabilities of the team. This will improve their ability to plan and prepare for tasks or projects.

9. Seek feedback and input from stakeholders: Seek feedback and input from relevant stakeholders, such as team members, clients, or other stakeholders, during the planning and preparation process. This can provide valuable insights, identify potential gaps, and help in refining the plan.

10. Continuously monitor and adjust: Continuously monitor the progress of the task or project and make necessary adjustments to the plan as needed. Regularly review and update the plan based on changing circumstances or new information to ensure that it remains effective and aligned with the objectives.

By implementing these strategies, you can effectively address the lack of planning and preparation, prevent failures from recurring, and increase the chances of success in future tasks or projects. Proper planning and preparation are crucial for setting a strong foundation for success and minimizing the risks of failure.

The strategies for identifying and addressing Inadequate Skills or Knowledge

When inadequate skills or knowledge are identified as a root cause of failure, it's important to take proactive steps to prevent it from recurring in the future. Here are some strategies to address the issue:

1. Conduct skills and knowledge assessment: Assess the skills and knowledge of team members involved in the task or project. Identify any gaps or deficiencies that may have contributed to the failure. This can be done through performance evaluations, skills assessments, or self-assessment questionnaires.

2. Provide training and development opportunities: Develop and implement training programs or workshops to address the identified skills or knowledge gaps. Provide team members with opportunities to enhance their skills and knowledge through relevant training,

workshops, certifications, or mentoring programs. This will improve their competency and effectiveness in executing tasks or projects.

3. Assign roles and responsibilities based on skills and expertise: Ensure that team members are assigned roles and responsibilities that align with their skills and expertise. Avoid assigning tasks or responsibilities that are beyond their capabilities, as it may result in inadequate performance and potential failure. Make sure team members have the necessary skills and knowledge to fulfill their assigned roles.

4. Foster a culture of continuous learning: Encourage a culture of continuous learning and improvement within the team or organization. Emphasize the importance of staying updated with industry trends, best practices, and new technologies. Provide resources and support for team members to engage in continuous learning, such as access to learning materials, online courses, or professional development opportunities.

5. Provide ongoing feedback and coaching: Regularly provide feedback and coaching to team members to help them improve their skills and knowledge. Provide constructive feedback on their performance, highlight areas for improvement, and offer guidance on how to enhance their skills. This will enable them to continually develop and grow their capabilities.

6. Encourage knowledge sharing and collaboration: Encourage team members to share their knowledge, insights, and best practices with each other. Foster a collaborative environment where team members can learn from each other and exchange ideas. Implement knowledge sharing platforms, regular team meetings, or peer-to-peer learning sessions to facilitate knowledge exchange.

7. Engage external expertise when needed: If the task or project requires specific skills or knowledge that the team does not possess, consider engaging external expertise. This could include hiring consultants, subject matter experts, or outsourcing certain tasks to qualified professionals. Leveraging external expertise can help address gaps in skills or knowledge and prevent failure.

8. Monitor progress and performance: Continuously monitor the progress and performance of team members in executing tasks or projects. Keep track of their performance against the desired outcomes and identify any potential skill or knowledge gaps that may arise during the course of the project. Take timely action to address any issues or gaps through appropriate interventions.

9. Encourage self-directed learning: Encourage team members to take ownership of their learning and development by engaging in self-directed learning. Provide resources and support for them to pursue self-directed learning opportunities, such as online courses, webinars, or self-paced learning materials. This will empower team members to proactively address their skill or knowledge gaps and prevent failure.

10. Conduct post-project reviews: After completing a project, conduct post-project reviews to reflect on the skills and knowledge required for success. Identify any gaps or deficiencies that may have contributed to the failure and incorporate those learnings into future projects. This will enable continuous improvement and prevent similar failures in the future.

By implementing these strategies, you can effectively identify and address inadequate skills or knowledge, prevent failures from recurring, and increase the chances of success in future tasks or projects. Developing a skilled and knowledgeable team is crucial for achieving project success and minimizing the risks of failure.

The strategies for identifying and addressing Poor Decision-making

Poor decision-making can often be a root cause of failure in various aspects of life, including personal and professional situations. Here are some strategies for identifying and addressing poor decision-making to prevent failure from recurring in the future:

1. Review decision-making processes: Evaluate the decision-making processes that were followed in the past, which led to failure. Identify any flaws, biases, or gaps in the decision-making process that may have resulted in poor decisions. Review the decision-making steps,

criteria, and factors that were considered, and assess their effectiveness in contributing to the failure.

2. Seek feedback and perspectives: Gather feedback from team members, stakeholders, or trusted advisors to gain insights into the decision-making process. Seek different perspectives and opinions to identify any potential blind spots or biases that may have influenced the poor decision-making. Encourage open and honest feedback to better understand the factors that contributed to the failure.

3. Identify decision-making triggers: Reflect on the triggers or situations that led to poor decision-making. Identify any recurring patterns or factors that influenced the decision-making process. For example, factors such as time pressure, lack of information, emotions, or personal biases can impact decision-making. Understanding these triggers can help prevent similar mistakes in the future.

4. Enhance decision-making skills: Invest in enhancing decision-making skills for individuals involved in the decision-making process. Provide training or resources to improve critical thinking, problem-solving, and analytical skills. Foster a culture that encourages sound decision-making based on data, facts, and evidence rather than emotions or personal biases.

5. Implement decision-making frameworks: Implement decision-making frameworks or models, such as SWOT analysis (Strengths, Weaknesses, Opportunities, and Threats), Pros and Cons analysis, or Decision Matrix, to guide the decision-making process. These frameworks provide a structured approach to decision-making, helping to minimize biases and ensure comprehensive consideration of relevant factors.

6. Foster collaboration and diversity of thought: Encourage collaboration and diversity of thought in the decision-making process. Involve multiple team members or stakeholders in the decision-making process to bring diverse perspectives, insights, and ideas to the table. This can help identify potential risks and opportunities that may not be apparent from a single perspective, leading to better decision-making.

7. Establish decision-making criteria: Define clear decision-making criteria based on the goals, objectives, and values of the organization or project. Establish criteria that align with the overall strategy and long-term vision. Use these criteria as a guideline for evaluating and selecting the best possible options.

8. Encourage reflection and learning: Foster a culture of reflection and learning from past decisions, both successes, and failures. Encourage team members to reflect on the outcomes of past decisions and learn from them. Conduct post-decision reviews to identify lessons learned and incorporate them into the decision-making process in the future.

9. Embrace experimentation and adaptability: Encourage a mindset of experimentation and adaptability in decision-making. Acknowledge that not all decisions will result in success and that adjustments may be needed along the way. Be open to changing course if new information or insights emerge, and be willing to learn from failures and adapt the decision-making approach accordingly.

10. Implement decision accountability measures: Establish accountability measures for decision-making. Clearly define roles and responsibilities for decision-making, and hold team members accountable for their decisions. Implement checks and balances to ensure that decisions are made based on proper processes, criteria, and considerations.

By implementing these strategies, you can identify and address poor decision-making, prevent failure from recurring in the future, and foster a culture of effective decision-making in your personal and professional endeavors. Effective decision-making is critical for achieving success and minimizing the risks of failure in any endeavor.

The strategies for identifying and addressing Fear of Taking Risks

Fear of taking risks can be a significant barrier to personal and professional growth, as it may prevent individuals from pursuing new opportunities or making bold decisions. Here are some strategies for identifying and addressing the fear of taking risks to prevent failure from recurring in the future:

1. Recognize and acknowledge fear: The first step in addressing fear of taking risks is to recognize and acknowledge it. Understand that fear is a natural emotion that everyone experiences to some extent. Accept and acknowledge your fears without judgment, and be willing to confront them head-on.

2. Understand the root causes of fear: Reflect on the underlying causes of your fear of taking risks. It could be related to past failures, negative experiences, lack of confidence, or fear of the unknown. Understanding the root causes of your fear can help you develop targeted strategies to address them.

3. Evaluate the risks and benefits: Conduct a thorough evaluation of the risks and benefits associated with the decision or opportunity at hand. Consider the potential outcomes, both positive and negative, and weigh them against each other. This rational evaluation can help you make informed decisions and reduce the impact of fear.

4. Develop a growth mindset: Cultivate a growth mindset, which is the belief that failures and setbacks are opportunities for learning and growth. Embrace a positive attitude towards failure as a stepping stone towards success. See risks as opportunities to stretch yourself, learn new skills, and gain valuable experiences.

5. Educate yourself and build skills: Acquire knowledge, skills, and information related to the decision or opportunity that you are considering. Educate yourself about the potential risks, challenges, and mitigation strategies. Building skills and knowledge can boost your confidence and reduce the fear associated with taking risks.

6. Plan and prepare: Proper planning and preparation can help minimize risks and uncertainties associated with taking risks. Develop a well-thought-out plan with clear goals, objectives, and strategies. Consider potential challenges and develop contingency plans. This level of preparedness can boost your confidence and reduce fear.

7. Start small and progress gradually: If the fear of taking risks is overwhelming, start with small steps and gradually progress towards bigger risks. This allows you to build confidence and develop

resilience along the way. Celebrate small successes, and use them as stepping stones towards bigger risks.

8. Surround yourself with support: Seek support from trusted friends, mentors, or colleagues. Surrounding yourself with a supportive network can provide encouragement, motivation, and perspective. They can also provide feedback and guidance, which can help you address your fears and take calculated risks.

9. Challenge negative thoughts and beliefs: Often, fear of taking risks is rooted in negative thoughts and limiting beliefs. Challenge these thoughts and beliefs by questioning their validity and rationality. Replace them with positive affirmations and empowering beliefs that support your ability to take risks and succeed.

10. Embrace failure as a learning opportunity: Shift your mindset to embrace failure as a learning opportunity rather than a reason to fear taking risks. Understand that failure is a natural part of the journey toward success, and it provides valuable lessons and feedback that can help you improve and grow.

By implementing these strategies, you can identify and address the fear of taking risks, prevent failure from recurring in the future, and empower yourself to pursue new opportunities with confidence and resilience. Taking calculated risks is often necessary for personal and professional growth, and overcoming the fear of risks can open up new possibilities and opportunities in your life.

The strategies for identifying and addressing Lack of Persistence and Resilience

Lack of persistence and resilience can be major factors that contribute to failure. It's important to develop strategies to identify and address these issues to prevent failure from recurring in the future. Here are some strategies to consider:

1. Reflect on the reasons for lack of persistence and resilience: Take the time to reflect on why you may lack persistence and resilience. Is it due to a lack of motivation, unclear goals, external challenges, or self-

doubt? Understanding the underlying reasons can help you develop targeted strategies to address them.

2. Set clear and meaningful goals: Clearly define your goals and make sure they are meaningful to you. Having a clear sense of purpose and direction can help you stay focused and motivated, even when faced with challenges or setbacks. Set realistic and achievable goals that are aligned with your values and aspirations.

3. Develop a growth mindset: Cultivate a growth mindset, which is the belief that challenges and setbacks are opportunities for learning and growth. Embrace a positive attitude towards failure and setbacks as valuable learning experiences that can strengthen your resilience and persistence.

4. Cultivate resilience: Resilience is the ability to bounce back from setbacks and adversity. Develop resilience by building a support system, practicing self-care, and developing coping strategies to manage stress and challenges. Learn from your failures and use them as opportunities to build resilience and adapt to changing circumstances.

5. Learn from failures: Embrace failure as a source of learning and improvement. Reflect on your failures and setbacks to identify the lessons learned and areas for improvement. Use these insights to adjust your approach and strategies, and apply the knowledge gained to prevent similar failures in the future.

6. Develop a plan for overcoming obstacles: Identify potential obstacles and challenges that may hinder your persistence and resilience. Develop a plan to address them proactively. This may include developing contingency plans, seeking support from others, or acquiring new skills or resources.

7. Practice self-compassion: Be kind to yourself and practice self-compassion when faced with failures or setbacks. Avoid self-blame or negative self-talk, and instead, practice self-encouragement and self-motivation. Treat yourself with the same kindness and understanding that you would offer to a friend facing similar challenges.

8. Seek feedback and guidance: Seek feedback from others, such as mentors, coaches, or trusted friends. Their perspectives and insights can provide valuable feedback on areas where you may need to improve your persistence and resilience. Don't be afraid to ask for help or guidance when needed.

9. Develop positive habits and routines: Establish positive habits and routines that support your persistence and resilience. This may include practicing regular exercise, mindfulness, or self-reflection. Having positive habits and routines can help you maintain focus, motivation, and resilience in the face of challenges.

10. Stay committed and keep going: Developing persistence and resilience requires consistent effort and determination. Stay committed to your goals and keep going, even when faced with challenges or setbacks. Remember that failure is a natural part of the journey towards success, and developing persistence and resilience can help you overcome obstacles and achieve your desired outcomes.

By implementing these strategies, you can identify and address lack of persistence and resilience, and prevent failure from recurring in the future. Building persistence and resilience is essential for overcoming challenges and setbacks, and it can significantly increase your chances of success in personal and professional endeavors.

The strategies for identifying and addressing Ineffective Communication and Collaboration

Ineffective communication and collaboration can be a common cause of failure in various personal and professional settings. Here are some strategies for identifying and addressing these issues to prevent failure from recurring in the future:

1. Improve active listening skills: Effective communication begins with active listening. Practice active listening by giving your full attention to the speaker, avoiding interruptions, asking clarifying questions, and summarizing the key points. This ensures that you understand the message accurately and helps to prevent miscommunication.

2. Enhance verbal and nonverbal communication skills: Verbal and nonverbal communication skills are critical in conveying messages clearly and effectively. Improve your verbal skills by using clear and concise language, avoiding jargon or technical terms, and adapting your communication style to the needs of your audience. Pay attention to your nonverbal cues such as body language, facial expressions, and tone of voice, as they can impact how your message is received.

3. Foster open and honest communication: Create a culture of open and honest communication where team members feel comfortable expressing their ideas, concerns, and feedback. Encourage open dialogue, active participation, and respectful communication among team members. This can help prevent misunderstandings and conflicts that can lead to failure.

4. Use the right communication channels: Choose the appropriate communication channels for different situations and audiences. Some messages may be better suited for face-to-face meetings, while others can be effectively communicated through emails, phone calls, or other digital tools. Using the right channels ensures that your messages are received and understood by the intended recipients.

5. Develop effective collaboration skills: Collaboration is key to success in many endeavors. Develop effective collaboration skills by fostering teamwork, building trust, and encouraging diversity of ideas and perspectives. Clearly define roles, responsibilities, and expectations, and establish effective channels for sharing information and feedback among team members.

6. Provide regular feedback: Feedback is crucial for continuous improvement. Provide regular feedback to team members on their communication and collaboration skills. Offer constructive feedback in a timely and respectful manner, highlighting areas for improvement and providing specific suggestions for how to enhance communication and collaboration.

7. Invest in training and development: Provide opportunities for team members to improve their communication and collaboration skills through training and development programs. Offer workshops,

seminars, or other learning opportunities that focus on effective communication, active listening, conflict resolution, and collaboration skills. Investing in training and development can help prevent communication and collaboration failures in the future.

8. Establish clear communication protocols: Establish clear communication protocols within your team or organization. Define guidelines for how communication should be conducted, including how information should be shared, how conflicts should be resolved, and how decisions should be made. Having clear communication protocols in place can help prevent misunderstandings and improve collaboration.

9. Foster a culture of feedback and continuous improvement: Encourage a culture of feedback and continuous improvement where team members are encouraged to provide feedback on communication and collaboration practices. Foster an environment where mistakes are seen as opportunities for learning and growth, and where team members are empowered to make suggestions for improving communication and collaboration.

10. Evaluate and adjust communication strategies: Regularly evaluate the effectiveness of your communication and collaboration strategies and make adjustments as needed. Monitor team dynamics, communication patterns, and outcomes to identify areas for improvement. Be willing to adapt and refine your communication strategies based on feedback and outcomes.

By implementing these strategies, you can identify and address ineffective communication and collaboration, and prevent failure from recurring in the future. Effective communication and collaboration are crucial for success in personal and professional settings, and investing in improving these skills can greatly enhance your chances of achieving your goals and preventing failures.

The strategies for identifying and addressing External Factors and Circumstances

External factors and circumstances can often impact our ability to achieve our goals and contribute to failure. Here are some strategies for identifying and addressing external factors and circumstances to prevent failure from recurring in the future:

1. Conduct a thorough analysis: Perform a comprehensive analysis of the external factors and circumstances that may have contributed to the failure. This may include factors such as market conditions, economic trends, regulatory changes, competition, technological disruptions, and other external influences. Identify the specific factors that played a role in the failure and assess their impact.

2. Stay informed and anticipate changes: Stay updated with the latest information and trends in your industry, market, or relevant external environment. Anticipate changes and proactively prepare for them. This may involve conducting regular market research, monitoring industry news and developments, engaging in professional networks, and seeking expert advice to stay informed and ahead of potential challenges.

3. Build contingency plans: Develop contingency plans to address potential external factors and circumstances that may impact your goals. Consider various scenarios and create plans to mitigate risks, adapt to changes, and take advantage of opportunities. Have backup strategies in place to minimize the impact of external factors on your goals and prevent failure.

4. Foster strategic partnerships: Build strategic partnerships and collaborations with other individuals, organizations, or stakeholders who can support your goals and help address external factors and circumstances. Collaborate with others to leverage their expertise, resources, and networks, and create synergies to navigate challenges and enhance your chances of success.

5. Develop adaptability and agility: Cultivate a mindset of adaptability and agility to respond to changing external circumstances. Be open to change, flexible in your approach, and willing to adjust your strategies and plans as needed. Develop the ability to quickly adapt to changing situations and make timely decisions to prevent failure.

Overcoming Failure

6. Diversify your resources: Diversify your resources, such as your customer base, product or service offerings, geographic markets, or revenue streams, to reduce dependence on any single external factor or circumstance. This can help you spread risk and minimize the impact of external factors on your goals.

7. Seek feedback and insights: Seek feedback from stakeholders, customers, partners, or other relevant sources to gain insights into potential external factors that may impact your goals. Listen to feedback, analyze insights, and use them to inform your strategies and decision-making. Be proactive in seeking feedback to stay informed and prepared.

8. Develop a proactive mindset: Develop a proactive mindset in addressing external factors and circumstances. Be proactive rather than reactive in your approach. Anticipate potential challenges, plan ahead, and take proactive measures to address them before they become significant barriers to your goals.

9. Monitor and evaluate regularly: Regularly monitor and evaluate the external factors and circumstances that may impact your goals. Keep a pulse on changes in the external environment and assess their impact on your strategies and plans. Make adjustments as needed to align with changing circumstances and prevent failure.

10. Learn from past failures: Reflect on past failures and learn from them. Identify any external factors or circumstances that contributed to the failure and use those lessons to inform your future strategies and decision-making. Leverage the knowledge gained from past failures to prevent similar failures from recurring in the future.

By implementing these strategies, you can identify and address external factors and circumstances that may contribute to failure and prevent them from recurring in the future. While external factors may be beyond our control, being proactive, adaptive, and strategic in addressing them can greatly improve your chances of success and mitigate the risk of failure.

The strategies for identifying and addressing Lack of Motivation and Focus

Lack of motivation and focus can significantly impact our ability to achieve our goals and contribute to failure. Here are some strategies for identifying and addressing lack of motivation and focus to prevent failure from recurring in the future:

1. Identify underlying causes: Take a deep dive into the root causes of your lack of motivation and focus. Reflect on why you may be struggling with motivation and focus. Is it due to external factors such as stress, burnout, or personal challenges? Or is it due to internal factors such as lack of passion, unclear goals, or lack of alignment with your values? Identifying the underlying causes can help you address them effectively.

2. Set clear and meaningful goals: Set clear, specific, and meaningful goals that are aligned with your values and aspirations. Goals that are personally meaningful and inspiring can boost your motivation and focus. Break down your goals into smaller, manageable tasks, and create a timeline to track your progress. Review your goals regularly to stay focused and motivated.

3. Create a compelling vision: Develop a compelling vision of what you want to achieve and why it matters to you. Visualize yourself achieving your goals and experiencing the rewards and benefits. This can create a sense of purpose and motivation to stay focused and committed to your goals, even when facing challenges.

4. Develop a plan and prioritize tasks: Create a well-defined plan with clear action steps to achieve your goals. Prioritize your tasks based on their importance and urgency. Break down complex tasks into smaller, achievable steps to make them more manageable. Having a plan in place can provide structure and guidance, helping you stay motivated and focused.

5. Find your intrinsic motivation: Tap into your intrinsic motivation, which comes from within, rather than relying solely on external motivators. Identify what truly inspires and motivates you, such as your passions, values, and personal aspirations. Align your goals and tasks with your intrinsic motivation to maintain sustained motivation and focus.

6. Eliminate distractions: Identify and eliminate distractions that hinder your motivation and focus. This may include distractions from technology, social media, negative influences, or other external factors. Create a conducive environment that minimizes distractions and promotes concentration and focus.

7. Develop healthy habits: Cultivate healthy habits that can boost your motivation and focus. This may include practicing good sleep hygiene, regular exercise, healthy eating, and stress management techniques. Taking care of your physical and mental well-being can enhance your motivation and focus, making you more resilient in the face of challenges.

8. Seek accountability and support: Seek accountability from a mentor, coach, or trusted colleague who can provide support and hold you accountable for your goals. Share your progress, challenges, and setbacks with them, and seek their guidance and encouragement. Having external support can help you stay motivated and focused, and provide valuable insights to address any obstacles.

9. Break tasks into smaller milestones: Breaking tasks into smaller, achievable milestones can provide a sense of progress and accomplishment, which can boost motivation and focus. Celebrate your milestones and reward yourself for your progress, which can further fuel your motivation to stay on track.

10. Practice self-reflection and self-awareness: Engage in regular self-reflection and self-awareness exercises to understand your thoughts, emotions, and behaviors. Be mindful of any patterns or triggers that may impact your motivation and focus negatively. Use self-awareness to make conscious choices and adjustments to maintain your motivation and focus.

By implementing these strategies, you can identify and address lack of motivation and focus, and prevent failure from recurring in the future. Cultivating a mindset of self-awareness, setting clear goals, developing a plan, eliminating distractions, and seeking support can help you maintain motivation and focus, and increase your chances of success. Remember, motivation and focus are key drivers of success, and addressing any issues in these areas

The strategies for identifying and addressing Inadequate Resource Management

Inadequate resource management can contribute to failure in various areas of life, including personal and professional endeavors. Here are some strategies for identifying and addressing inadequate resource management to prevent failure from recurring in the future:

1. Assess current resource utilization: Take a comprehensive inventory of the resources you currently have and how they are being utilized. This includes financial resources, time, human capital, technology, and other relevant resources. Evaluate how efficiently and effectively you are utilizing these resources towards your goals. Identify any areas where resources are being underutilized or mismanaged.

2. Identify resource gaps: Identify any gaps or deficiencies in your resource management. Are there any critical resources that are lacking or insufficient for your goals? Are there any areas where you need additional resources or support to prevent failure? Assessing the gaps in your resource management can help you pinpoint areas that require improvement.

3. Develop a resource management plan: Create a comprehensive plan for managing your resources effectively. This may include budgeting and financial planning, time management, human resource allocation, technology optimization, and other relevant areas. Develop strategies and action steps for each resource category to ensure efficient and effective utilization.

4. Prioritize resources based on goals: Prioritize your resources based on the goals you want to achieve. Allocate resources in a way that aligns with your strategic priorities and objectives. Avoid spreading your resources too thin across multiple goals, as this can lead to inadequate resource management and increased risk of failure.

5. Seek expert advice and support: Seek expert advice and support in managing specific resources that you may not have sufficient expertise in. For example, consulting with a financial advisor for financial resource management, or seeking input from a project manager for

human resource allocation. Utilizing external expertise can help you optimize your resource management strategies and prevent failure.

6. Monitor and track resource utilization: Regularly monitor and track the utilization of your resources to ensure that they are being used efficiently and effectively. Review and analyze data and feedback to identify any gaps or areas for improvement. Make adjustments to your resource management plan as needed based on performance metrics and feedback.

7. Implement resource optimization techniques: Explore and implement resource optimization techniques to maximize the utilization of your resources. This may include techniques such as automation, outsourcing, delegation, and process improvement. Look for opportunities to streamline resource allocation and utilization to prevent waste or inefficiencies.

8. Develop contingency plans: Develop contingency plans for handling unexpected changes or disruptions in resource availability. This may include having backup plans for financial emergencies, alternative resource options in case of shortages, or contingency plans for managing unexpected delays or disruptions. Having contingency plans in place can help you mitigate risks and prevent failure.

9. Foster a culture of resource management: Foster a culture of resource management within your team or organization. Educate and empower team members to manage resources effectively in their respective areas of responsibility. Encourage a proactive approach to resource management and provide the necessary tools and training for team members to optimize their resource utilization.

10. Continuously improve resource management practices: Continuously evaluate and improve your resource management practices over time. Regularly review and reflect on your resource management strategies and outcomes. Look for opportunities to learn from failures or challenges and implement improvements to prevent similar issues from recurring in the future.

By implementing these strategies, you can identify and address inadequate resource management to prevent failure from recurring in the future. Effective resource management can significantly impact your success in achieving your goals and mitigating risks of failure. Remember to assess your current resource utilization, identify gaps, develop a resource management plan, prioritize resources, seek expert advice, monitor utilization, implement optimization techniques, develop contingency plans, foster a culture of resource management, and continuously improve your practices to optimize your resource management and increase your chances of success.

The strategies for identifying and addressing Personal Limitations and Mindset

Personal limitations and mindset can be significant factors that contribute to failure in various aspects of life. Here are some strategies for identifying and addressing personal limitations and mindset to prevent failure from recurring in the future:

1. Self-awareness: Develop self-awareness by reflecting on your thoughts, emotions, and behaviors. Identify any personal limitations or negative mindsets that may be hindering your progress towards your goals. This may include self-doubt, limiting beliefs, negative self-talk, or fixed mindset. Be honest with yourself and strive to gain a deep understanding of your personal limitations and mindset patterns.

2. Seek feedback: Seek feedback from trusted friends, mentors, or colleagues to gain an external perspective on your personal limitations and mindset. Ask for specific feedback on areas where you may need improvement or areas where your mindset may be holding you back. Be open to feedback and willing to make changes based on the feedback received.

3. Challenge limiting beliefs: Challenge and reframe any limiting beliefs that may be holding you back. Identify any negative or self-limiting beliefs that may be influencing your thoughts and behaviors in a detrimental way. Replace them with more positive, empowering beliefs that support your goals and aspirations. Practice positive self-talk and cultivate a growth mindset, which is the belief that you can develop your abilities and intelligence through effort and learning.

Overcoming Failure

4. Develop new skills and competencies: Identify any skills or competencies that may be limiting your progress towards your goals. Take proactive steps to develop new skills or improve existing ones. This may involve seeking training, education, or mentorship to enhance your capabilities and overcome personal limitations.

5. Set realistic goals: Set realistic and achievable goals that align with your abilities and current mindset. Avoid setting overly ambitious goals that may set you up for failure and reinforce negative mindsets. Start with small, manageable goals that are within your reach and gradually work your way towards more challenging goals as you build confidence and competence.

6. Practice self-compassion: Be compassionate towards yourself and recognize that failure is a part of the learning process. Avoid harsh self-criticism or self-blame for past failures. Instead, practice self-compassion by acknowledging your efforts, learning from mistakes, and treating yourself with kindness and understanding. Use failures as opportunities for growth and learning rather than dwelling on them as a reflection of your self-worth.

7. Cultivate a growth mindset: Cultivate a growth mindset, which is the belief that your abilities and intelligence can be developed through effort and learning. Embrace challenges and setbacks as opportunities for growth and learning. Emphasize the process of learning and improvement rather than focusing solely on outcomes or results. Embrace a positive, proactive, and adaptable mindset that fosters continuous learning and improvement.

8. Surround yourself with positive influences: Surround yourself with positive influences such as supportive friends, mentors, or colleagues who inspire and motivate you. Avoid negative influences or environments that may reinforce limiting beliefs or negative mindsets. Surrounding yourself with positive influences can help you stay motivated, focused, and aligned with your goals.

9. Practice self-reflection and journaling: Regularly practice self-reflection and journaling to identify and address any personal limitations or mindset patterns that may be hindering your progress.

Write down your thoughts, emotions, and behaviors related to your goals, failures, and challenges. Reflect on your experiences, thoughts, and emotions to gain insights into your personal limitations and mindset. Use journaling as a tool for self-awareness, self-reflection, and personal growth.

10. Seek support and accountability: Seek support from mentors, coaches, or accountability partners who can provide guidance, encouragement, and motivation. Share your goals, challenges, and progress with them and seek their input and feedback. Having external support and accountability can help you stay focused, motivated, and committed to addressing your personal limitations and mindset. They can provide insights, perspectives, and suggestions for overcoming personal limitations and improving your mindset. Regular check-ins with your support system can help you stay on track and make necessary adjustments to prevent failure from recurring in the future.

Remember, addressing personal limitations and mindset is a continuous process that requires self-awareness, effort, and dedication. Be patient with yourself, and don't be afraid to seek help when needed. With consistent effort and the right strategies, you can overcome personal limitations, cultivate a positive mindset, and prevent failure from recurring in the future.

Chapter 3: Cultivating Resilience in the Face of Failure

Resilience is the ability to bounce back from setbacks, and it's a critical skill in overcoming failure.

How to cultivate resilience by developing mental and emotional toughness

Cultivating resilience, or the ability to bounce back from setbacks and challenges, is essential for overcoming failures and achieving personal and professional success. Resilience is not something that is innate or fixed, but rather, it can be developed and strengthened over time. One key aspect of resilience is developing mental and emotional toughness, which involves building a strong mindset and emotional regulation skills. Here are some strategies to cultivate resilience by developing mental and emotional toughness:

1. Practice self-awareness: Self-awareness is the foundation of resilience. It involves being aware of your thoughts, emotions, and behaviors, and understanding how they impact your resilience. Take time to reflect on your thoughts and emotions in challenging situations. Are you engaging in negative self-talk? Are you letting fear or stress control your emotions? By being aware of your mental and emotional responses, you can begin to develop a more resilient mindset.

2. Reframe failure as an opportunity for growth: Rather than viewing failure as a permanent setback, reframe it as an opportunity for learning and growth. Embrace a growth mindset, which believes that failures are not final, but rather, they provide valuable feedback and learning experiences. When you encounter failure, ask yourself what you can learn from it and how you can use it to improve and grow stronger.

3. Develop effective coping strategies: Resilient individuals have effective coping strategies to deal with stress and adversity. These can include relaxation techniques such as deep breathing, mindfulness, exercise, or engaging in activities that you enjoy. Experiment with different coping strategies and identify what works best for you in managing stress and building mental and emotional toughness.

4. Build a support system: Having a support system of friends, family, mentors, or colleagues can greatly contribute to your resilience. Surround yourself with individuals who provide emotional support, encouragement, and guidance during difficult times. Don't be afraid to reach out and seek help when needed. Having a strong support system can provide a sense of belonging and help you navigate challenges with greater resilience.

5. Develop emotional regulation skills: Resilient individuals have the ability to regulate their emotions effectively, even in the face of challenges. Practice emotional regulation skills, such as identifying and expressing your emotions in a healthy and constructive way, managing stress and anxiety, and developing a positive outlook. These skills can help you stay calm, focused, and resilient during difficult times.

6. Foster a positive mindset: Cultivating a positive mindset involves focusing on the positives, practicing gratitude, and reframing negative thoughts into more positive and constructive ones. Develop a habit of looking for the silver lining in challenging situations and practicing positive self-talk. A positive mindset can help you maintain optimism and resilience in the face of setbacks.

7. Set realistic goals and take action: Setting realistic goals and taking action towards them can boost your self-confidence and resilience. Break down your goals into smaller, manageable steps, and take consistent action towards them. Celebrate your progress, no matter how small, and use it as motivation to keep moving forward.

8. Learn from setbacks and mistakes: View setbacks and mistakes as opportunities for learning and growth. Reflect on what went wrong, what could have been done differently, and how you can improve in the future. Avoid dwelling on self-blame or guilt, and instead focus on learning from the experience and applying those lessons in your future endeavors.

Cultivating resilience by developing mental and emotional toughness is a proactive process that requires self-awareness, effective coping strategies, a positive mindset, and a support system. By practicing these strategies, you can strengthen your resilience and navigate challenges with greater confidence, adaptability, and success.

How to cultivate resilience by building a support system

Building a support system is a crucial component of cultivating resilience, as it provides individuals with a network of people who can offer emotional support, guidance, and encouragement during challenging times. Here are some strategies for building a support system to cultivate resilience:

1. Identify your support needs: Reflect on what kind of support you need during difficult times. It could be emotional support, practical advice, or simply someone to lend a listening ear. Understanding your support needs will help you identify the right people to include in your support system.

2. Seek out diverse sources of support: A well-rounded support system includes different types of relationships and people from various aspects of your life. This can include close friends, family members, mentors, colleagues, or members of a support group or community. Consider reaching out to individuals who bring different perspectives, experiences, and strengths to your support system.

3. Communicate openly and honestly: Building a supportive relationship requires open and honest communication. Share your thoughts, emotions, and challenges with your support system, and be willing to listen and receive feedback. Avoid bottling up your emotions or pretending that everything is fine, as this can hinder the development of a genuine and effective support system.

4. Nurture healthy relationships: Building a support system involves nurturing healthy relationships based on trust, mutual respect, and understanding. Invest time and effort in maintaining these relationships, and show appreciation and gratitude for the support you receive. Be willing to reciprocate and offer support to others in your support system as well.

5. Set healthy boundaries: While support from others is valuable, it's important to set healthy boundaries to protect your own well-being. Be

clear about your needs, expectations, and limitations. Communicate your boundaries with respect and assertiveness, and be willing to say no when necessary. Setting healthy boundaries helps prevent potential issues or dependencies that could hinder your resilience.

6. Seek professional help when needed: In some cases, building a support system may involve seeking professional help from therapists, counselors, or coaches. These individuals are trained to provide specialized support and guidance during difficult times. Don't hesitate to seek professional help when needed, as it can be a crucial component of cultivating resilience.

7. Foster mutual support: Building a support system is not just about receiving support, but also about providing support to others. Foster a culture of mutual support within your relationships by actively listening, showing empathy, and offering assistance when appropriate. Being there for others can also contribute to your own resilience, as it fosters a sense of purpose and fulfillment.

8. Practice reciprocity: Just as you receive support from your support system, be willing to reciprocate and offer support to others when needed. Providing support to others not only strengthens your relationships but also contributes to your own resilience by fostering a sense of connection, empathy, and altruism.

Building a support system is an essential strategy for cultivating resilience. By identifying your support needs, seeking diverse sources of support, communicating openly, nurturing healthy relationships, setting boundaries, seeking professional help when needed, fostering mutual support, and practicing reciprocity, you can build a robust support system that helps you navigate challenges with greater resilience, strength, and well-being.

How to cultivate resilience by maintaining a positive outlook despite failure.

Maintaining a positive outlook despite failure is a crucial aspect of cultivating resilience. It involves developing a mindset that allows you to see failures as opportunities for growth and learning, rather than as insurmountable obstacles.

Here are some strategies for cultivating resilience by maintaining a positive outlook despite failure:

1. Practice self-compassion: It's important to be kind and compassionate to yourself when you experience failure. Avoid self-blame, self-criticism, or negative self-talk, as these can undermine your resilience. Instead, practice self-compassion by treating yourself with the same kindness, understanding, and support that you would offer to a friend facing a similar situation. Acknowledge your emotions, validate your experience, and offer yourself words of encouragement and comfort.

2. Reframe failure as an opportunity for learning: Rather than viewing failure as a defeat, reframe it as an opportunity for learning and growth. Embrace a growth mindset that sees failure as a natural part of the learning process and an opportunity to gain valuable insights, skills, and experience. Reflect on what you can learn from the failure, what you could have done differently, and how you can apply those lessons in future endeavors.

3. Focus on the positives: Instead of dwelling on the negatives or what went wrong, shift your focus to the positives. Identify and celebrate any small wins, achievements, or progress that you made, even in the face of failure. Cultivate gratitude by acknowledging the things in your life that are going well and the opportunities that are still available to you. Focusing on the positives can help shift your perspective and maintain a positive outlook despite failure.

4. Practice optimistic thinking: Cultivate optimistic thinking by reframing negative thoughts and beliefs into more positive and constructive ones. Challenge and replace negative or self-defeating thoughts with more realistic and optimistic ones. For example, instead of thinking "I'm a failure," reframe it as "I experienced a setback, but I can learn from it and improve." Practice positive self-talk and visualization techniques to reinforce a positive outlook.

5. Surround yourself with positive influences: Surrounding yourself with positive influences, such as supportive friends, mentors, or role models, can help you maintain a positive outlook despite failure. Seek out individuals who inspire and motivate you, and spend time with

them. Avoid negative or toxic influences that can bring you down or reinforce negative beliefs about failure. Surrounding yourself with positive influences can help you maintain a positive perspective and mindset.

6. Engage in self-care: Taking care of your physical, mental, and emotional well-being is essential for maintaining a positive outlook despite failure. Engage in self-care activities that promote relaxation, self-reflection, and self-nurturing. This can include exercise, mindfulness, meditation, journaling, or engaging in hobbies or activities that bring you joy and fulfillment. Taking care of yourself holistically can boost your resilience and help you maintain a positive outlook.

7. Set realistic expectations: Failure can be particularly discouraging when it's accompanied by unrealistic expectations. Set realistic expectations for yourself and your goals, recognizing that setbacks and failures are a normal part of life. Avoid placing excessive pressure or demands on yourself, as this can increase the likelihood of disappointment and negativity. Set achievable goals and celebrate progress, even if it's incremental.

Maintaining a positive outlook despite failure is crucial for cultivating resilience. By practicing self-compassion, reframing failure as an opportunity for learning, focusing on the positives, practicing optimistic thinking, surrounding yourself with positive influences, engaging in self-care, and setting realistic expectations, you can develop a mindset that enables you to bounce back from failure with resilience, optimism, and a positive outlook.

Practical techniques for coping with failure and turning it into a stepping stone towards success

Coping with failure and turning it into a stepping stone towards success involves developing practical techniques that can help you navigate through the challenges and setbacks of failure, and use them as opportunities for growth and learning. Here are some practical techniques for coping with failure and turning it into a stepping stone towards success:

1. Practice self-reflection: Take the time to reflect on the failure and understand what went wrong. Identify the factors that contributed to the failure, including your own actions, decisions, and mindset. Be honest with yourself and avoid blaming others or making excuses. Self-reflection can help you gain insights and learn from your mistakes, which can inform your future actions and decisions.

2. Adjust your mindset: Adopting a growth mindset can be a powerful technique for coping with failure. Embrace the belief that failure is a natural part of the learning process and an opportunity for growth. See failure as a chance to learn, improve, and develop resilience. Reframe failure as a stepping stone towards success, rather than a roadblock.

3. Set realistic goals: Setting realistic and achievable goals can help you cope with failure and prevent setting yourself up for disappointment. Evaluate your goals and ensure they are realistic, measurable, and attainable. Break larger goals into smaller, more manageable steps, and celebrate progress along the way. Setting realistic goals can help you stay focused and motivated, even in the face of failure.

4. Learn from failure: Failure can provide valuable lessons and insights that can inform your future actions and decisions. Take the time to identify what you have learned from the failure and how you can apply those lessons in future endeavors. Consider failure as a feedback mechanism that helps you improve and grow. Use the knowledge and experience gained from failure to make informed decisions and take calculated risks in the future.

5. Seek support: It's important to have a support system in place to cope with failure. Reach out to trusted friends, mentors, or colleagues for emotional support, encouragement, and advice. Surround yourself with individuals who can offer perspective, guidance, and insights. Seeking support can help you gain a fresh perspective, process your emotions, and develop coping strategies.

6. Take action: After reflecting on the failure and learning from it, take action toward your goals. Avoid dwelling on failure or getting stuck in a cycle of negativity. Develop a plan of action, set specific tasks and deadlines, and take steps towards your goals. Taking action can help

you regain a sense of control and momentum, and turn failure into a driving force toward success.

7. Practice resilience: Resilience is the ability to bounce back from failure and adversity. Cultivate resilience by developing mental and emotional toughness, and by maintaining a positive outlook despite failure. Practice self-compassion, positive self-talk, and optimistic thinking. Keep a perspective that failure is a temporary setback and not a reflection of your worth or abilities. Embrace challenges as opportunities for growth and keep moving forward.

8. Embrace perseverance: Success often requires perseverance and persistence, especially in the face of failure. Embrace a mindset of perseverance and view failure as a temporary setback that does not define your journey toward success. Stay committed to your goals, remain focused, and keep taking action despite setbacks. Perseverance can help you overcome obstacles and turn failure into a stepping stone toward success.

Coping with failure and turning it into a stepping stone towards success involves adopting a growth mindset, setting realistic goals, learning from failure, seeking support, taking action, practicing resilience, and embracing perseverance. By applying these practical techniques, you can develop the resilience and determination needed to navigate through failure, learn from it, and use it as an opportunity to move forward towards success.

Chapter 4: Learning from Failure: Extracting Valuable Lessons

Failure can be a valuable source of learning and growth if we know how to extract lessons from it.

What are the processes of learning from failure?

The process of learning from failure involves several key steps that can help you gain insights, identify areas for improvement, and use failure as a catalyst for growth and success. Here are the key steps in the process of learning from failure:

1. Reflect: Take the time to reflect on the failure and the circumstances surrounding it. Consider the factors that contributed to the failure, including your own actions, decisions, and mindset. Be honest with yourself and avoid blaming others or making excuses. Reflect on what happened, why it happened, and what could have been done differently.

2. Identify lessons learned: Once you have reflected on the failure, identify the lessons learned. What insights and knowledge have you gained from the experience? What mistakes were made, and what can be done differently in the future? Be specific and objective in identifying the lessons learned, and avoid being overly self-critical or negative. Focus on constructive feedback and actionable insights.

3. Analyze root causes: Dig deeper into the root causes of the failure. Identify the underlying factors that led to the failure, such as inadequate planning, lack of skills or knowledge, poor decision-making, external factors, or personal limitations. Understanding the root causes can help you address the underlying issues and prevent similar failures in the future.

4. Develop an action plan: Based on the lessons learned and the analysis of root causes, develop an action plan for improvement. Identify specific actions and steps that can be taken to address the areas for improvement. Set clear and measurable goals, establish deadlines, and create a roadmap for implementation. Be proactive and committed to taking action to address the issues identified.

5. Seek feedback: Seek feedback from others, such as mentors, colleagues, or trusted individuals, to gain additional perspectives on the failure and potential areas for improvement. Listen to feedback with an open mind and be willing to receive constructive criticism. Feedback from others can provide valuable insights and help you gain a different perspective on the failure and potential solutions.

6. Implement changes: Take action on your action plan and implement the changes identified. Be consistent and committed to making the necessary changes based on the lessons learned. Monitor your

progress, track your results, and adjust your approach as needed. Be patient with yourself and recognize that change takes time and effort.

7. Reflect and iterate: Continuously reflect on your progress and results, and iterate your approach as needed. Keep learning, adapting, and improving based on the feedback and results you receive. Embrace a mindset of continuous improvement and be open to new insights and opportunities for growth.

8. Apply learnings in the future: As you move forward, apply the lessons learned from the failure in your future endeavors. Use the knowledge and experience gained to make informed decisions, take calculated risks, and prevent similar failures from occurring in the future. Incorporate the insights and improvements into your ongoing practices and strategies.

Learning from failure is a continuous process that requires self-reflection, analysis, action, feedback, and a commitment to ongoing improvement. By following these steps, you can leverage failure as a valuable opportunity for learning and growth, and ultimately use it as a stepping stone towards future success.

How to identify the lessons learned from failure and how to apply them to future endeavors for improved outcomes.

Identifying the lessons learned from failure and applying them to future endeavors is a critical step in the process of learning from failure and using it as a stepping stone towards improved outcomes. Here are some practical steps to help you identify lessons learned from failure and apply them to future endeavors:

1. Reflect on the failure: Take the time to reflect on the failure and the circumstances surrounding it. Consider the factors that contributed to the failure, including your actions, decisions, and mindset. Be honest with yourself and avoid blaming others or making excuses. Reflect on what happened, why it happened, and what could have been done differently.

2. Analyze root causes: Dig deeper into the root causes of the failure. Identify the underlying factors that led to the failure, such as inadequate planning, lack of skills or knowledge, poor decision-making, external factors, or personal limitations. Understanding the root causes can help you identify the areas for improvement and prevent similar failures in the future.

3. Extract key insights: Based on your reflection and analysis, extract key insights and lessons learned from the failure. What knowledge, skills, or perspectives have you gained from the experience? What mistakes were made, and what can be done differently in the future? Be specific and objective in identifying the lessons learned, and focus on actionable insights that can be applied in future endeavors.

4. Create an action plan: Develop an action plan for applying the lessons learned to future endeavors. Identify specific actions and steps that can be taken to incorporate the lessons learned into your decision-making, planning, and execution. Set clear and measurable goals, establish deadlines, and create a roadmap for implementation. Be proactive and committed to taking action on the lessons learned.

5. Monitor progress: As you implement the action plan, monitor your progress and results. Keep track of how you are applying the lessons learned in your future endeavors and evaluate the outcomes. Be honest with yourself and assess whether the changes you have made based on the lessons learned are leading to improved outcomes.

6. Adjust and iterate: Based on the feedback and results you receive, adjust and iterate your approach as needed. Be open to new insights and feedback from others, and be willing to adapt your strategies and actions. Embrace a mindset of continuous improvement and be proactive in making changes to improve your future endeavors based on the lessons learned from failure.

7. Embrace a growth mindset: Cultivate a growth mindset, which is characterized by a willingness to learn, adapt, and improve. Embrace failures as opportunities for learning and growth, and view them as stepping stones towards improved outcomes in the future. Avoid a

fixed mindset, which may lead to a fear of failure and reluctance to take risks.

8. Incorporate lessons learned into ongoing practices: Finally, incorporate the lessons learned from failure into your ongoing practices and strategies. Use the knowledge and experience gained to inform your decision-making, planning, and execution in future endeavors. Apply the insights and improvements in a deliberate and intentional manner to prevent similar failures from occurring and to increase the likelihood of success in the future.

By following these steps, you can identify the lessons learned from failure and apply them to future endeavors for improved outcomes. It requires self-reflection, analysis, action, monitoring, and a growth mindset to effectively learn from failure and use it as a springboard towards success in the future.

Chapter 5: Overcoming the Fear of Failure

Fear of failure can be a significant barrier to success.

What are the root causes of fear of failure?

Fear of failure can arise from various root causes, and it may vary from person to person. Here are some common root causes of fear of failure:

1. Past negative experiences: Previous failures or negative experiences can create a fear of failure. If someone has experienced significant setbacks or failures in the past, they may develop a fear of repeating those experiences, which can lead to a reluctance to take risks or try new things.

2. High stakes or consequences: When the stakes are high or the potential consequences of failure are perceived as severe, it can lead to fear of failure. For example, in situations where significant financial, professional, or personal consequences are at stake, the fear of failing and facing those consequences can be overwhelming.

3. Unrealistic expectations: Unrealistic or perfectionistic expectations of oneself or from others can contribute to fear of failure. When there is excessive pressure to meet high standards or achieve unattainable goals, the fear of falling short and not meeting those expectations can create anxiety and fear of failure.

4. Fear of judgment or criticism: Fear of being judged or criticized by others can also lead to fear of failure. The fear of what others may think or say if one fails can create anxiety and reluctance to take risks or try new things for fear of being judged negatively by others.

5. Low self-esteem or self-worth: Low self-esteem or self-worth can also contribute to fear of failure. When someone has a negative self-perception or lacks confidence in their abilities, they may fear failure as it can reinforce negative beliefs about themselves or their worthiness.

6. Lack of confidence or skills: When someone lacks confidence in their abilities or skills required for a task or goal, it can lead to fear of

failure. The fear of not being competent enough to succeed can create anxiety and avoidance of taking risks or pursuing new opportunities.

7. Perceived loss of control: Fear of failure can also stem from a perceived loss of control. If someone feels that failure would result in a loss of control over their circumstances or life, it can trigger fear and anxiety.

8. Cultural or societal factors: Cultural or societal factors can also contribute to fear of failure. Societal or cultural norms that place a high emphasis on success, achievement, or perfection can create fear of failure as it may be associated with shame, guilt, or negative social consequences.

It's important to note that fear of failure is a natural emotion that many people experience to varying degrees. However, understanding the root causes of fear of failure can help individuals identify and address them, develop coping strategies, and cultivate a healthier relationship with failure. It may involve developing self-confidence, setting realistic expectations, reframing perceptions of failure, challenging negative beliefs, seeking support, and gradually facing and overcoming fears through exposure and practice.

Practical strategies for overcoming it

Overcoming the fear of failure requires a conscious effort and a willingness to challenge and change one's mindset. Here are some practical strategies that can help:

1. Reframe failure as a learning opportunity: Instead of viewing failure as something negative, reframe it as an opportunity to learn and grow. Embrace failure as a natural part of the learning process and a stepping stone towards success. Recognize that failure can provide valuable feedback, insights, and lessons that can inform future endeavors.

2. Set realistic expectations: Unrealistic expectations of perfection can fuel fear of failure. Set realistic and achievable goals for yourself, acknowledging that setbacks and failures may happen along the way. Avoid setting overly high standards that are difficult to meet, and allow room for mistakes and setbacks as part of the learning process.

3. Challenge negative beliefs: Identify and challenge any negative beliefs or thought patterns related to failure. Often, fear of failure is fueled by irrational beliefs such as "Failure is unacceptable," "Failure defines my worth," or "Failure is catastrophic." Replace these negative beliefs with more rational and constructive thoughts, such as "Failure is a normal part of life," "Failure does not define my worth as a person," or "Failure provides an opportunity to learn and improve."

4. Cultivate self-compassion: Practice self-compassion and kindness towards yourself when facing failure. Treat yourself with the same kindness and understanding that you would offer to a friend who has experienced failure. Avoid self-blame, self-criticism, or negative self-talk, and instead practice self-encouragement, self-acceptance, and self-support.

5. Build a support system: Surround yourself with a supportive network of friends, family, mentors, or colleagues who can offer encouragement, guidance, and feedback. Share your failures and challenges with them, and seek their support and perspective. Having a support system can provide emotional resilience and help you maintain a positive outlook despite failures.

6. Develop resilience and coping skills: Cultivate resilience by developing coping skills that can help you manage stress, anxiety, and setbacks. This may include mindfulness techniques, deep breathing exercises, physical exercise, journaling, or seeking professional support from a therapist or counselor. Building resilience can help you bounce back from failures and setbacks with greater emotional strength and adaptability.

7. Take gradual risks and build confidence: Gradually expose yourself to risks and challenges, and celebrate small successes along the way. This can help you build confidence in your abilities and gradually desensitize yourself to the fear of failure. Break down larger goals into smaller, manageable steps, and take incremental risks to build your confidence and competence.

8. Learn from past failures: Reflect on past failures and identify the lessons learned from them. What went wrong? What could you have

done differently? How can you apply those lessons to future endeavors for improved outcomes? Use failures as opportunities for self-reflection, self-assessment, and personal growth.

Remember that overcoming the fear of failure is a process and may require consistent effort and practice. It's important to be patient with yourself and be willing to step out of your comfort zone to face and address your fears. With time and practice, you can develop a healthier mindset towards failure and use it as a stepping stone towards success.

Reframing failure

Reframing failure refers to changing one's perspective or mindset about the concept of failure in a more positive and constructive way. Instead of viewing failure as something negative or as a final outcome, reframing involves looking at failure as a learning opportunity, a chance to grow, and a stepping stone towards success. It involves shifting from a negative or defeatist mindset to a more positive and proactive one.

Reframing failure can involve changing how we interpret, perceive, and respond to failure. It involves recognizing that failure is a normal part of life and that everyone experiences failure at some point. It's not something to be ashamed of or avoid, but rather an opportunity for growth and improvement.

Here are some key aspects of reframing failure:

1. Learning opportunity: Failure can be viewed as a valuable learning opportunity. It can provide insights, feedback, and lessons that can inform future endeavors and help us make better decisions in the future. Instead of dwelling on the negative aspects of failure, reframing involves focusing on the potential learning and growth that can come from it.

2. Growth mindset: Embracing a growth mindset, which is the belief that our abilities and intelligence can be developed through effort and learning, can help reframe failure. With a growth mindset, failure is seen as a temporary setback rather than a permanent state. It encourages a proactive approach of learning, adapting, and improving after experiencing failure.

3. Resilience: Reframing failure involves cultivating resilience, which is the ability to bounce back from setbacks and adversity. It's about developing emotional strength, adaptability, and perseverance in the face of failure. Resilience helps us view failure as a challenge to be overcome rather than an insurmountable obstacle.

4. Perspective: Reframing failure involves changing our perspective on failure. Instead of seeing failure as a reflection of our worth as a person or defining us as a failure, it's about recognizing that failure is a normal part of life and does not define our value or potential. It's about seeing failure as a temporary event or outcome, rather than a permanent state.

5. Positive mindset: Reframing failure involves maintaining a positive outlook despite failure. It's about focusing on the lessons learned, the progress made, and the potential for future success. It involves avoiding self-blame, negative self-talk, or dwelling on the past, and instead cultivating a positive and forward-looking mindset.

Reframing failure requires conscious effort and practice. It may not come naturally, as we are often conditioned to view failure negatively. However, with intentional effort, we can shift our mindset and develop a more positive and constructive perspective on failure, which can ultimately lead to personal growth, resilience, and improved outcomes in future endeavors.

Developing a growth mindset

Developing a growth mindset involves cultivating a belief that our abilities and intelligence can be developed through effort, learning, and perseverance. It is a mindset that embraces challenges, views failures as opportunities for learning, and seeks continuous improvement. Developed by psychologist Carol Dweck, the concept of a growth mindset has gained significant attention in the fields of psychology, education, and personal development.

Here are key aspects of developing a growth mindset:

1. Embracing challenges: A growth mindset involves embracing challenges and seeing them as opportunities for growth, rather than as threats or obstacles. It's about being willing to step outside of one's

comfort zone and take on new and challenging tasks, even if they may initially seem difficult or daunting.

2. Viewing failures as learning opportunities: With a growth mindset, failures are seen as part of the learning process. Instead of being discouraged or giving up, individuals with a growth mindset view failures as opportunities to learn, improve, and grow. They see failures as feedback that helps them understand where they need to improve and adjust their approach.

3. Cultivating a love for learning: Developing a growth mindset involves cultivating a love for learning and a curiosity to acquire new knowledge and skills. It's about being open to new ideas, seeking out learning opportunities, and being willing to invest time and effort in acquiring new knowledge and improving oneself.

4. Emphasizing effort and perseverance: A growth mindset emphasizes the importance of effort and perseverance in achieving success. It recognizes that skills and abilities can be developed through persistent effort and dedication over time. It encourages individuals to embrace challenges, put in consistent effort, and persevere in the face of setbacks or obstacles.

5. Changing self-talk and beliefs: Developing a growth mindset involves changing self-talk and beliefs from fixed to growth-oriented. It's about replacing negative self-talk, such as "I'm not good at this" or "I'll never be able to do it," with more positive and constructive self-talk, such as "I can improve with effort and practice" or "This is an opportunity for me to learn and grow."

6. Fostering a positive learning environment: Developing a growth mindset is also influenced by the environment in which one learns and grows. A positive learning environment, such as supportive and encouraging teachers, mentors, or peers, can foster a growth mindset by promoting a culture of learning, effort, and improvement.

Developing a growth mindset takes time and effort, and it may require challenging and changing deeply ingrained beliefs and attitudes. However, it can lead to a more resilient, adaptive, and proactive mindset that promotes personal growth, learning, and success in various aspects of life.

Building self-confidence to face failure with courage and resilience.

Building self-confidence is an important aspect of facing failure with courage and resilience. When we are confident in ourselves and our abilities, we are better equipped to handle failures and setbacks with resilience and determination. Here are some key points to understand about building self-confidence in the face of failure:

1. Self-awareness: Building self-confidence starts with self-awareness, which involves understanding our strengths, weaknesses, values, and beliefs. It's important to have a clear understanding of our abilities, skills, and areas for improvement. Knowing ourselves well allows us to set realistic expectations, leverage our strengths, and work on areas that need improvement.

2. Positive self-talk and mindset: Our inner dialogue, or self-talk, plays a significant role in our self-confidence. It's important to develop a positive self-talk and mindset that reinforces our self-worth, acknowledges our efforts and progress, and reframes failures as learning opportunities. Avoiding negative self-talk and self-sabotaging beliefs can help us build self-confidence and face failure with resilience.

3. Setting and achieving realistic goals: Setting and achieving realistic goals can boost our self-confidence. When we set attainable goals and work towards them, we build a sense of accomplishment and self-efficacy. It's important to break larger goals into smaller, manageable steps, celebrate progress along the way, and learn from setbacks or failures to improve our approach in the future.

4. Building on past successes: Reflecting on past successes, big or small, can help build self-confidence. It reminds us of our capabilities and achievements, and provides us with a positive reference point when facing challenges or failures. By acknowledging our past successes, we can foster a belief in our ability to overcome challenges and achieve future successes.

5. Continuous learning and improvement: Building self-confidence involves a mindset of continuous learning and improvement. Embracing a growth mindset, as discussed earlier, means seeing failures as opportunities for learning and improvement. By seeking feedback, learning from mistakes, and continuously improving ourselves, we can build self-confidence and resilience to face failures.

6. Surrounding oneself with a supportive network: Having a supportive network of friends, mentors, or colleagues can greatly impact our self-confidence. Surrounding ourselves with people who believe in us, provide encouragement, and offer constructive feedback can boost our self-confidence and provide us with a support system to lean on during challenging times.

7. Practicing self-care: Taking care of our physical and mental well-being is essential in building self-confidence. Prioritizing self-care, such as getting enough sleep, eating well, managing stress, and engaging in activities that bring joy and relaxation, can contribute to a positive mindset and increased self-confidence.

Building self-confidence is a gradual process that requires effort, self-awareness, and practice. It's important to remember that failure is a natural part of life, and facing it with courage, resilience, and self-confidence can help us learn, grow, and ultimately succeed in our endeavors.

Chapter 6: Failing Forward: Turning Failure into Success

Concept of "failing forward

"Failing forward" is a concept that emphasizes viewing failure as a stepping stone towards progress and growth. It suggests that failures should not be seen as final setbacks, but rather as opportunities for learning, improvement, and future success. The concept of "failing forward" encourages individuals to adopt a positive and proactive mindset towards failure, rather than fearing or avoiding it.

The idea of "failing forward" suggests that failures can provide valuable feedback, insights, and experiences that can help individuals learn, adapt, and make better choices in the future. Instead of dwelling on the negative aspects of failure, "failing forward" encourages individuals to embrace failure as a part of the learning process and to use it as a catalyst for growth and development.

Here are some key aspects of the concept of "failing forward":

1. Learning from failure: "Failing forward" emphasizes the importance of actively learning from failure. This includes reflecting on what went wrong, identifying areas for improvement, and making necessary adjustments to prevent similar failures in the future. Failure can provide valuable lessons and insights that can be applied to future endeavors for improved outcomes.

2. Taking calculated risks: "Failing forward" recognizes that failure can be a result of taking risks, and encourages individuals to take calculated risks in pursuit of their goals and aspirations. It emphasizes the importance of stepping out of one's comfort zone, trying new things, and being willing to accept failure as a possible outcome in the pursuit of growth and progress.

3. Resilience and perseverance: "Failing forward" acknowledges that failure can be challenging and discouraging, but it encourages individuals to bounce back from failures with resilience and perseverance. It emphasizes the importance of not giving up, but rather

using failures as motivation to keep pushing forward towards one's goals.

4. Seeing failure as feedback, not finality: "Failing forward" encourages individuals to reframe their perception of failure from being a final defeat to being feedback on what can be improved. It emphasizes that failure does not define an individual's worth or potential, but rather provides valuable information on what can be done differently in the future.

5. Embracing a growth mindset: "Failing forward" aligns with the concept of a growth mindset, which is the belief that abilities and intelligence can be developed through effort, learning, and perseverance. It encourages individuals to view failure as an opportunity to grow and develop new skills, rather than a fixed outcome that determines their abilities or potential.

Overall, "failing forward" promotes a positive and proactive approach towards failure, encouraging individuals to embrace failure as a part of the learning process, learn from it, and use it as a stepping stone towards future success. It emphasizes the importance of resilience, learning, and continuous improvement, and encourages individuals to maintain a positive and proactive mindset in the face of failures.

Reframing failure as an opportunity for growth

Reframing failure as an opportunity for growth involves shifting one's perspective and mindset towards failure, seeing it as a valuable learning experience rather than a negative outcome. Here are some practical strategies for reframing failure as an opportunity for growth:

1. Embrace a growth mindset: Adopt a growth mindset, which is the belief that abilities and intelligence can be developed through effort, learning, and perseverance. Emphasize the idea that failure is not a reflection of one's worth or potential, but rather an opportunity to learn, improve, and grow.

2. Change the language around failure: Instead of using negative language when referring to failure, reframe it using more positive and

empowering language. For example, instead of saying "I failed," say "I learned valuable lessons." This can help shift the focus from failure as a negative outcome to failure as a source of learning and growth.

3. Reflect on the lessons learned: Take time to reflect on what went wrong, what could have been done differently, and what can be learned from the experience. Identify the key lessons or insights that can be gained from the failure, and use them as a foundation for making better choices and decisions in the future.

4. Focus on the process, not just the outcome: Instead of solely focusing on the outcome of failure, shift your attention to the process and effort put forth. Recognize and celebrate the effort, courage, and resilience demonstrated, regardless of the outcome. This can help build a sense of accomplishment and self-efficacy, even in the face of failure.

5. Set realistic expectations: Understand that failure is a natural part of the learning process and that everyone experiences it at some point. Set realistic expectations for yourself and acknowledge that setbacks and failures are opportunities for growth and improvement, rather than reasons for self-criticism or self-doubt.

6. Look for silver linings: Train yourself to look for the silver linings in failure. For example, failure can highlight areas for improvement, uncover hidden weaknesses, or reveal new opportunities that may not have been apparent before. Try to see failure as a catalyst for positive change and growth, rather than a defeat.

7. Seek support and feedback: Reach out to trusted mentors, colleagues, or friends for support and feedback. Getting different perspectives and insights can provide new insights and help reframe failure in a more constructive light. Surrounding yourself with a supportive network can also help boost your resilience and motivation to bounce back from failure.

8. Take action and move forward: Avoid dwelling on failure or getting stuck in a negative mindset. Instead, take action and use the lessons learned from failure to make positive changes and move forward. Take

proactive steps towards improvement and growth, and use the failure as a driving force to motivate you towards future success.

By reframing failure as an opportunity for growth, you can shift your mindset and perspective towards failure in a more positive and constructive way. This can help you approach failure with resilience, curiosity, and a willingness to learn, ultimately leading to personal and professional growth.

Leveraging failure to gain new insights and skills

Leveraging failure to gain new insights and skills involves actively using the experience of failure as a valuable source of learning and growth. Here are some steps you can take to leverage failure for gaining new insights and skills:

1. Reflect on the failure: Take time to reflect on the failure and analyze what happened, what went wrong, and what could have been done differently. Be honest with yourself and try to identify the root causes or contributing factors that led to the failure. This reflection can provide valuable insights and help you understand the underlying issues that need to be addressed or improved upon.

2. Identify learning opportunities: Look for the silver linings in the failure by identifying the learning opportunities it presents. Ask yourself what you can learn from the experience, what new knowledge or skills you can acquire, and how you can apply these lessons to future endeavors. Be open to feedback from others and use it as a source of learning and growth.

3. Embrace a growth mindset: Adopt a growth mindset, which is the belief that abilities and intelligence can be developed through effort, learning, and perseverance. Emphasize the idea that failure is not a reflection of your worth or potential, but rather an opportunity to learn, improve, and grow. Embrace challenges and view failure as a stepping stone towards success, rather than a dead-end.

4. Take calculated risks: Use failure as a motivation to take calculated risks and step out of your comfort zone. Failure can provide important feedback on what works and what doesn't, helping you make more informed decisions and take calculated risks in the future. Be willing to

try new things, experiment with different approaches, and learn from the outcomes, whether they are successes or failures.

5. Seek feedback and guidance: Seek feedback from others, such as mentors, colleagues, or experts, to gain new perspectives and insights. Be open to constructive criticism and feedback, and use it as an opportunity to identify areas for improvement and acquire new skills. Consider seeking guidance or mentorship from those who have experience in the areas where you have faced failure, as they can provide valuable advice and guidance for overcoming challenges and improving your skills.

6. Practice resilience and perseverance: Failure can be emotionally challenging, but it's important to practice resilience and perseverance. Recognize that failure is a part of the learning process and that setbacks are inevitable in any pursuit of success. Embrace failure as a temporary setback and keep pushing forward, using the lessons learned to make better decisions and take more informed actions.

7. Take action and apply the lessons learned: Use the insights and skills gained from the failure to take action and make positive changes. Apply the lessons learned to your future endeavors, implementing new strategies, approaches, or skills acquired from the failure. Be proactive in applying the insights gained and take intentional steps towards improvement and growth.

By leveraging failure as an opportunity for gaining new insights and skills, you can turn setbacks into valuable learning experiences that contribute to your personal and professional growth. Embrace a growth mindset, seek feedback, reflect on the failure, take calculated risks, practice resilience, and apply the lessons learned to your future endeavors, using failure as a stepping stone towards success.

Using failure as a catalyst for innovation and creativity.

Failure can serve as a catalyst for innovation and creativity when approached with the right mindset and strategies. Here are some ways to use failure as a catalyst for innovation and creativity:

1. Embrace a growth mindset: Adopt a growth mindset that views failure as an opportunity for learning and growth, rather than a setback or a reflection of your abilities. Emphasize the idea that failure is a natural part of the innovation and creativity process and that it can provide valuable feedback and insights for improvement.

2. Foster a culture of experimentation: Create an environment that encourages experimentation, where failure is seen as a stepping stone towards innovation and creativity. Encourage team members to take risks, try new ideas, and explore different approaches, even if they may result in failure. Celebrate the process of learning and experimentation, rather than solely focusing on outcomes.

3. Learn from failure: Reflect on failures and analyze what went wrong, what could have been done differently, and what can be learned from the experience. Encourage open and honest discussions about failures, and use them as opportunities for collective learning. Encourage team members to share their failures, insights, and lessons learned with the rest of the team, and use these as building blocks for future innovations and creative solutions.

4. Encourage creativity and divergent thinking: Failure can spark creativity and divergent thinking by pushing individuals and teams to think outside the box and explore unconventional solutions. Encourage brainstorming, ideation sessions, and creative problem-solving techniques to generate new ideas and approaches. Emphasize the importance of looking beyond traditional solutions and encourage experimentation and iteration to foster innovation.

5. Foster collaboration and diverse perspectives: Collaboration and diverse perspectives can lead to innovative solutions. Encourage teamwork and collaboration among team members, and create opportunities for cross-functional collaboration and diverse perspectives. Encourage team members to share their unique perspectives and insights, and leverage the collective knowledge and skills of the team to identify new approaches and solutions.

6. Encourage iterative experimentation: Use failure as a stepping stone towards iterative experimentation. Encourage team members to iterate

on their ideas and solutions, making incremental improvements based on the insights gained from failures. Foster a culture of continuous improvement and encourage team members to view failures as opportunities to iterate, refine, and innovate further.

7. Provide resources and support: Provide the necessary resources, tools, and support for team members to experiment, innovate, and learn from failure. This may include providing training, mentorship, access to relevant information and expertise, and a supportive environment where team members feel empowered to take risks and learn from failures.

By embracing a growth mindset, fostering a culture of experimentation, learning from failure, encouraging creativity and divergent thinking, fostering collaboration and diverse perspectives, promoting iterative experimentation, and providing necessary resources and support, failure can be used as a catalyst for innovation and creativity. When failures are seen as learning opportunities and used to fuel new ideas, approaches, and solutions, they can contribute to the development of innovative and creative solutions that drive success in the long run.

Examples of individuals who have turned their failures into success stories.

There are numerous real-life examples of individuals who have turned their failures into success stories. Here are a few notable examples:

1. Walt Disney: Walt Disney, the legendary creator of Disney World and Disneyland, faced multiple failures and setbacks before achieving success. He was fired from a job at a newspaper for "lack of creativity" and experienced failed business ventures. However, he persevered and continued to pursue his passion for animation, eventually creating iconic characters like Mickey Mouse and building a global entertainment empire.

2. Steve Jobs: Steve Jobs, the co-founder of Apple Inc., faced failure early in his career when he was ousted from Apple, the company he co-founded. However, he used that setback as an opportunity to start new ventures, including NeXT Inc. and Pixar Animation Studios, which eventually led to his return to Apple and the development of

revolutionary products like the iPhone and iPad, making Apple one of the most valuable and influential technology companies in the world.

3. Oprah Winfrey: Oprah Winfrey, a media mogul, philanthropist, and talk show host, faced significant challenges in her early life, including poverty, abuse, and discrimination. However, she persevered, and through hard work, determination, and resilience, she built a successful media empire that includes the Oprah Winfrey Show, a successful television network (OWN), and various philanthropic efforts.

4. J.K. Rowling: J.K. Rowling, the renowned author of the Harry Potter series, faced numerous rejections from publishers before finding success. Her initial manuscript for Harry Potter was rejected by multiple publishers, but she did not give up. She persevered, kept refining her work, and eventually secured a publishing deal that led to the unprecedented success of the Harry Potter series, making her one of the wealthiest and most influential authors in the world.

5. Michael Jordan: Michael Jordan, widely considered one of the greatest basketball players of all time, faced failures and setbacks early in his career. He was cut from his high school basketball team, faced challenges in college, and experienced playoff losses in his early NBA career. However, he used these setbacks as motivation to work harder, improve his skills, and eventually became a global icon and a highly successful athlete, winning six NBA championships and earning numerous awards and accolades.

These are just a few examples of individuals who faced failures but turned them into success stories by leveraging their resilience, determination, and perseverance. They refused to give up, learned from their failures, and used them as stepping stones towards achieving their goals and dreams. Their stories illustrate the power of resilience, positive mindset, and determination in overcoming failures and achieving success.

Chapter 7: Persevering Through Failure: The Power of Grit

Grit, the combination of passion and perseverance, is a key trait that can help us overcome failure.

Concept of grit and its role in overcoming failure

Grit is a psychological trait that refers to a combination of perseverance, resilience, passion, and determination to achieve long-term goals, even in the face of challenges, setbacks, and failures. It is often associated with the ability to persist in pursuing goals and to bounce back from failures, and it plays a crucial role in overcoming failure and achieving success.

Here are some key points about grit and its role in overcoming failure:

1. Resilience: Grit enables individuals to bounce back from failures and setbacks. It helps them to persevere and maintain their motivation and determination, even when faced with obstacles and disappointments. Resilience is essential in the face of failure, as it allows individuals to learn from their mistakes, adapt, and keep moving forward, rather than being discouraged or giving up.

2. Perseverance: Grit involves a high level of perseverance, which is the ability to keep working towards a goal despite difficulties and obstacles. When facing failure, individuals with grit are more likely to keep trying, keep learning, and keep improving, rather than being deterred by setbacks. They understand that failure is a part of the process and a stepping stone towards success.

3. Passion: Grit is fueled by passion, which is a strong and enduring emotional attachment to one's goals and pursuits. Passion provides the motivation and drive to keep going, even when the going gets tough. When individuals are truly passionate about their goals, they are more likely to persevere through failures and setbacks, as they have a deep emotional investment in their endeavors.

4. Learning mindset: Gritty individuals view failures as opportunities for learning and growth. They embrace a learning mindset, constantly

seeking feedback, analyzing failures, and extracting valuable lessons from them. They use failures as stepping stones to improve, refine their strategies, and make better decisions in the future. They see failure as a temporary setback, rather than a reflection of their worth or abilities.

5. Goal-oriented focus: Gritty individuals maintain a strong focus on their long-term goals, despite the challenges they may face along the way. They understand that failure is not the end of the journey but rather a temporary setback. They keep their eyes on the bigger picture, and they are willing to put in the effort, time, and energy needed to achieve their goals, regardless of the failures they may encounter.

In summary, grit plays a crucial role in overcoming failure by fostering resilience, perseverance, passion, a learning mindset, and a goal-oriented focus. It enables individuals to bounce back from setbacks, learn from failures, and keep moving forward towards their goals, ultimately increasing their chances of achieving success.

Strategies for developing grit

Developing grit, or cultivating resilience, perseverance, passion, and a learning mindset, can be achieved through several strategies. Here are some practical strategies for developing grit:

1. Set meaningful goals: Identify long-term goals that are personally meaningful and align with your values and interests. Having a clear sense of purpose and direction can provide the motivation and drive needed to persevere through challenges and setbacks.

2. Cultivate a growth mindset: Embrace a mindset that views failures and setbacks as opportunities for learning and growth, rather than as personal shortcomings or failures. Adopt a positive attitude towards failure and see it as a chance to gain insights, develop new skills, and improve in the future.

3. Build resilience: Strengthen your ability to bounce back from failures and setbacks by developing resilience. Practice coping skills such as problem-solving, emotion regulation, and stress management. Build a

support system of friends, family, mentors, or coaches who can provide encouragement and guidance during difficult times.

4. Develop perseverance: Cultivate a "never give up" attitude by developing perseverance. Recognize that achieving meaningful goals takes time and effort, and setbacks are a natural part of the process. Be willing to persist and keep trying, even when faced with challenges or failures.

5. Foster passion: Cultivate a sense of passion and enthusiasm for your goals. Connect with the emotional aspect of your pursuits and remind yourself why you are passionate about them. When you have a deep emotional investment in your goals, you are more likely to persevere through failures and setbacks.

6. Learn from failures: Embrace a learning mindset towards failures. Reflect on your failures, analyze what went wrong, and identify valuable lessons that can inform your future actions. Use failures as an opportunity to gain insights, refine your strategies, and make better decisions in the future.

7. Maintain a goal-oriented focus: Keep your long-term goals in sight and maintain a goal-oriented focus. Stay committed to your goals, even when faced with obstacles or failures. Break down your goals into smaller, manageable steps, and celebrate small successes along the way to stay motivated.

8. Practice self-compassion: Be kind and compassionate towards yourself when facing failures. Avoid self-blame or negative self-talk, and instead, practice self-compassion. Treat yourself with the same kindness, understanding, and support that you would offer to a friend facing similar challenges.

9. Cultivate patience and perseverance: Recognize that developing grit takes time and effort. It is a skill that can be developed and strengthened through practice and persistence. Be patient with yourself and embrace the process of building grit, knowing that it is a lifelong journey.

Incorporating these strategies into your mindset and behaviors can help you develop grit and cultivate resilience, perseverance, passion, and a learning mindset. Remember that developing grit is a gradual process, and it may take time and effort, but the benefits of increased resilience and perseverance in the face of failure can greatly contribute to your success in various areas of life.

Chapter 8: Managing Emotions and Rebuilding Self-Worth after Failure

Failure can be emotionally challenging, and it's essential to manage our emotions effectively to overcome it.

Strategies for managing emotions

Managing emotions such as disappointment, frustration, and self-doubt after experiencing failure can be challenging, but there are several strategies that can help:

1. Acknowledge and validate emotions: It's important to acknowledge and validate the emotions you're experiencing after failure. Allow yourself to feel disappointed, frustrated, or doubtful without judging or criticizing yourself. Remember that it's okay to feel these emotions and that they are a natural part of the human experience.

2. Practice self-awareness: Cultivate self-awareness by paying attention to your thoughts, feelings, and behaviors related to the failure. Notice any patterns or triggers that may be contributing to your emotional response. Being aware of your emotions can help you better manage them and respond in a constructive manner.

3. Express emotions in healthy ways: Find healthy outlets to express your emotions, such as talking to a trusted friend, writing in a journal, or engaging in physical activity. Avoid suppressing or denying your emotions, as this can lead to them festering and becoming more challenging to manage.

4. Challenge negative thoughts: Notice and challenge any negative thoughts or self-doubt that may arise after failure. Practice cognitive reframing, which involves identifying and replacing negative or unhelpful thoughts with more realistic and constructive ones. This can help you shift your perspective and manage self-doubt more effectively.

5. Practice self-compassion: Treat yourself with kindness, understanding, and self-compassion after experiencing failure. Be gentle with yourself

and avoid harsh self-criticism or self-blame. Remember that failure is a part of life, and everyone experiences it at some point. Treat yourself with the same compassion and understanding that you would offer to a friend in a similar situation.

6. Reframe failure as a learning opportunity: Embrace a growth mindset and view failure as a valuable learning opportunity. Recognize that failures can provide insights, feedback, and opportunities for growth and improvement. Reframe failure as a stepping stone towards success and use it as a chance to learn, adapt, and move forward.

7. Practice self-care: Take care of yourself physically, mentally, and emotionally. Get enough sleep, eat nutritious meals, engage in regular exercise, and practice relaxation techniques such as deep breathing or meditation. Taking care of your overall well-being can help you better manage emotions and build resilience.

8. Seek support: Don't be afraid to seek support from others, whether it's from friends, family, mentors, or a therapist. Talking about your emotions and experiences with others can provide validation, perspective, and helpful insights. Surround yourself with a supportive network that can offer encouragement and guidance during challenging times.

9. Set realistic expectations: Recognize that failure is a part of life, and setbacks are inevitable. Set realistic expectations for yourself and others, and avoid placing undue pressure or perfectionism on yourself. Accept that failures are opportunities for growth and learning, and that they do not define your worth or potential for future success.

By practicing these strategies, you can better manage emotions such as disappointment, frustration, and self-doubt that may arise after failure. Remember that managing emotions is a skill that can be developed and improved over time with practice and self-awareness. Be patient with yourself, and give yourself the space and support needed to process and manage your emotions in a healthy and constructive manner.

Techniques for rebuilding self-worth and restoring confidence in ourselves

Experiencing failure can often impact our self-worth and confidence, but there are techniques that can help rebuild self-worth and restore confidence. Here are some techniques:

1. Practice self-compassion: Treat yourself with kindness, understanding, and self-compassion. Recognize that everyone makes mistakes and experiences failure at some point in life. Be gentle with yourself and avoid harsh self-criticism or self-blame. Offer yourself the same empathy and understanding that you would offer to a friend in a similar situation.

2. Challenge negative self-talk: Notice and challenge any negative self-talk that may arise after failure. Replace self-defeating thoughts with more realistic and constructive ones. Practice positive self-affirmation and remind yourself of your strengths, accomplishments, and capabilities. Avoid engaging in negative self-comparison or dwelling on perceived failures.

3. Reflect on lessons learned: Instead of dwelling on the failure itself, focus on the lessons learned from it. Reflect on what went wrong, what could have been done differently, and what you can learn from the experience. View failure as an opportunity for growth and improvement, and use the insights gained to make better choices in the future.

4. Set realistic goals: Set realistic and achievable goals for yourself, taking into consideration the lessons learned from failure. Break down larger goals into smaller, manageable steps, and celebrate progress along the way. Setting realistic goals and achieving them can help rebuild self-worth and boost confidence.

5. Focus on strengths and accomplishments: Shift your focus from the failure to your strengths and accomplishments. Remind yourself of your past successes, achievements, and positive feedback from others. Engage in activities that you enjoy and that make you feel competent and confident. Surround yourself with people who uplift and support you.

6. Practice self-care: Take care of yourself physically, mentally, and emotionally. Prioritize self-care by getting enough sleep, eating nutritious meals, engaging in regular exercise, and practicing stress management techniques. Taking care of your overall well-being can help restore your confidence and sense of self-worth.

7. Cultivate a growth mindset: Embrace a growth mindset, which involves viewing failure as an opportunity for learning and growth. Recognize that failures are not indicative of your worth or potential, but rather as stepping stones towards success. Embrace challenges as opportunities to develop new skills, gain experience, and expand your capabilities.

8. Seek support: Don't be afraid to seek support from others, whether it's from friends, family, mentors, or a therapist. Talking about your feelings and experiences with others can provide validation, perspective, and helpful insights. Surround yourself with a supportive network that can offer encouragement and guidance as you rebuild your self-worth and restore confidence.

Rebuilding self-worth and restoring confidence after experiencing failure takes time and effort. It's important to be patient with yourself and practice self-compassion along the way. Remember that failure is a normal part of life, and it doesn't define your worth or potential. By practicing these techniques and focusing on self-care, self-compassion, and a growth mindset, you can rebuild your self-worth and restore your confidence in yourself.

Chapter 9: Navigating Failure in Different Areas of Life

Failure can occur in various areas of our lives, including relationships, career, health, and personal goals.

Navigating failure in different areas of life

Failure can happen in various areas of life, such as personal relationships, career, academics, health, and other pursuits. Navigating failure in different areas of life may require different strategies, but here are some general tips that can help:

1. Acknowledge and accept failure: The first step in navigating failure is to acknowledge and accept it as a part of life. Recognize that everyone experiences failure at some point, and it's a natural part of the learning and growth process. Avoid denying or ignoring failure, as this can hinder your ability to move forward.

2. Allow yourself to feel and process emotions: Failure can evoke a range of emotions, such as disappointment, frustration, sadness, anger, or fear. It's important to allow yourself to feel and process these emotions in a healthy way. Give yourself permission to experience and express your emotions without judgment or suppression, and seek support from trusted individuals if needed.

3. Reflect on the failure and learn from it: Reflect on the failure and try to gain insights from it. Consider what went wrong, what could have been done differently, and what can be learned from the experience. Use the failure as an opportunity for growth and learning, and apply the lessons learned to future endeavors.

4. Reframe failure as an opportunity: Reframe failure as an opportunity for growth, rather than a permanent setback. Adopt a positive and constructive mindset that views failure as a chance to learn, improve, and become more resilient. Embrace the idea that failure can lead to new opportunities and possibilities.

5. Develop a plan for moving forward: Create a plan for how to move forward after failure. Set realistic and achievable goals, break them down into smaller steps, and create an action plan. Identify resources,

strategies, and support systems that can help you overcome the failure and work towards your goals.

6. Practice self-care: Taking care of yourself is crucial when navigating failure. Practice self-care by taking time for self-reflection, engaging in activities that bring you joy and relaxation, getting enough sleep, eating well, and managing stress. Taking care of your physical and mental well-being can help you cope with failure and maintain resilience.

7. Seek support: Don't be afraid to seek support from others. Talk to trusted friends, family, mentors, or professionals about your experience and feelings. Seek guidance, encouragement, and perspective from others who can provide a fresh outlook and offer support as you navigate through failure.

8. Stay persistent and resilient: Failure can be discouraging, but it's important to stay persistent and resilient. Stay committed to your goals, and don't let failure define you or deter you from pursuing your aspirations. Embrace a growth mindset and be willing to learn, adapt, and persevere in the face of failure.

9. Practice self-compassion: Be kind and compassionate towards yourself as you navigate failure. Avoid self-blame, self-criticism, and negative self-talk. Treat yourself with the same kindness, understanding, and empathy that you would offer to a friend. Practice self-compassion as you process and learn from failure.

10. Learn from other's experiences: Finally, learn from the experiences of others who have navigated failure. Seek inspiration from stories of individuals who have faced and overcome failure in similar areas of life. Learn from their strategies, perspectives, and insights to help you navigate your own failure.

Remember, failure is a part of life, and it's how we respond to it that can shape our growth and success. By acknowledging, accepting, and learning from failure, developing a constructive mindset, seeking support, and practicing self-care and self-compassion, you can navigate failure in different areas of life and come out stronger on the other side.

How the strategies for overcoming failure may vary depending on the context.

The strategies for overcoming failure may vary depending on the context in which the failure occurs. Different areas of life, such as career, relationships, academics, health, and personal pursuits, may require different approaches to effectively navigate and overcome failure. Here are some examples of how strategies for overcoming failure may vary depending on the context:

1. Career: In the context of a career, failure may involve setbacks such as not getting a job promotion, a project not going as planned, or a business venture not succeeding. Strategies for overcoming career-related failure may involve reflection on the specific factors that contributed to the failure, identifying areas for improvement, seeking feedback from mentors or colleagues, and developing new skills or strategies to enhance professional growth. Networking, seeking additional education or training, and exploring new opportunities or career paths may also be relevant strategies in the context of career-related failure.

2. Relationships: Failure in relationships, such as a breakup, a conflict, or a falling out with a friend or family member, may require strategies that focus on communication, empathy, and reconciliation. Strategies for overcoming relationship-related failure may involve reflecting on the dynamics and contributing factors of the relationship, communicating openly and honestly with the other party, seeking support from trusted individuals, and working towards repairing or rebuilding the relationship through active listening, understanding, and forgiveness.

3. Academics: Failure in the context of academics, such as poor grades, not meeting academic goals, or struggling with a course, may require strategies that involve academic support, time management, and study skills. Strategies for overcoming academic failure may involve seeking academic assistance, such as tutoring or additional resources, setting realistic goals and developing a study plan, improving study habits, and seeking guidance from professors or mentors to identify areas for improvement and develop a plan for academic success.

4. Health: Failure in the context of health, such as not achieving health goals, experiencing setbacks in fitness or wellness pursuits, or facing health challenges, may require strategies that focus on self-care, self-compassion, and seeking appropriate medical support. Strategies for overcoming health-related failure may involve reassessing health goals, developing a realistic and sustainable plan for improving health, seeking guidance from healthcare professionals, and practicing self-care and self-compassion as one navigates health challenges or setbacks.

5. Personal pursuits: Failure in personal pursuits, such as hobbies, creative endeavors, or personal goals, may require strategies that involve self-reflection, perseverance, and creativity. Strategies for overcoming failure in personal pursuits may involve reflecting on the specific factors that contributed to the failure, identifying areas for improvement or creative solutions, seeking inspiration from others or trying new approaches, and developing a resilient mindset that embraces the learning and growth opportunities inherent in failure.

It's important to note that the strategies for overcoming failure are not one-size-fits-all, and may need to be tailored to the specific context in which the failure occurs. The key is to approach failure with a growth mindset, be willing to learn from the experience and adapt strategies as needed to effectively navigate and overcome failure in the specific context in which it arises.

Practical tips and techniques for bouncing back from failure in different areas of our lives and continuing to pursue our dreams.

Bouncing back from failure and continuing to pursue our dreams requires resilience, determination, and a growth mindset. Here are some practical tips and techniques that can help in different areas of life:

1. Acknowledge and process emotions: Failure can trigger a range of emotions, such as disappointment, frustration, and self-doubt. It's important to acknowledge and process these emotions in a healthy way. Allow yourself to feel and express the emotions, but avoid dwelling on them or suppressing them. Find healthy outlets, such as talking to a trusted friend or family member, writing in a journal, or

seeking professional support, to help process and manage your emotions effectively.

2. Reflect and learn from failure: Failure can provide valuable insights and opportunities for growth. Reflect on the specific factors that contributed to the failure and identify areas for improvement. Ask yourself what you could have done differently, what you learned from the experience, and how you can apply those lessons to future endeavors. Embrace failure as a learning opportunity and a stepping stone towards success.

3. Reframe failure as an opportunity: Reframe your perspective on failure by viewing it as an opportunity for growth and improvement, rather than as a setback. Shift your mindset from a fixed mindset that sees failure as a reflection of your worth or abilities, to a growth mindset that sees failure as a chance to learn, adapt, and become better. Embrace a positive and constructive outlook towards failure, and use it as a catalyst for innovation and creativity.

4. Set realistic goals and develop a plan: After experiencing failure, it's important to set realistic goals and develop a plan to move forward. Break down your goals into smaller, manageable steps and create a roadmap for achieving them. Set realistic expectations and avoid putting unnecessary pressure on yourself. Having a plan in place can help you stay focused and motivated as you work towards your dreams.

5. Seek support: Surround yourself with a supportive network of friends, family, mentors, or colleagues who can provide encouragement, guidance, and feedback. Don't be afraid to ask for help when needed. Supportive individuals can offer different perspectives, insights, and advice that can help you gain new insights and approach challenges from different angles. Additionally, seeking professional support, such as coaching, therapy, or counseling, can be beneficial in navigating failure and building resilience.

6. Practice self-compassion: Treat yourself with kindness, understanding, and self-compassion after experiencing failure. Avoid self-blame or harsh self-criticism, and instead, practice self-compassion by acknowledging that failure is a part of the human experience and that

everyone encounters setbacks at some point. Be gentle with yourself, practice self-care, and practice positive self-talk to boost your self-esteem and restore your confidence.

7. Stay persistent and resilient: Bouncing back from failure requires persistence and resilience. It's important to stay committed to your dreams and not give up. Accept that failure is a part of the journey toward success and that setbacks are temporary. Stay focused on your goals, stay resilient in the face of challenges, and keep moving forward with determination and perseverance.

8. Embrace innovation and creativity: Failure can be an opportunity to think outside the box and explore new approaches. Embrace innovation and creativity by trying new strategies, exploring different perspectives, and thinking creatively about how to overcome challenges. Be open to new ideas and perspectives, and be willing to adapt and iterate your approach as needed.

9. Cultivate self-belief and confidence: Building self-belief and confidence is crucial in bouncing back from failure. Remind yourself of your strengths, achievements, and capabilities. Focus on your past successes and use them as a source of motivation and inspiration. Surround yourself with positive influences and engage in activities that boost your self-esteem. Developing a strong sense of self-belief and confidence can help you rebuild your self-worth and restore your confidence in yourself, despite experiencing failure.

10. Take action and persevere: After experiencing failure, it's important to take action and keep moving forward. Avoid getting stuck in a cycle of negative thoughts or self-doubt. Take small, meaningful steps towards your goals, even if they are baby steps. Celebrate small victories along the way and stay persistent in your efforts. Remember that failure is not the end, but rather a stepping stone towards success.

11. Practice resilience and adaptability: Resilience and adaptability are key traits that can help you bounce back from failure in different areas of life. Cultivate resilience by developing the ability to bounce back from setbacks, learn from challenges, and keep going despite obstacles. Be adaptable by being open to change, willing to learn from failure, and

Overcoming Failure

flexible in your approach. Embrace a mindset of continuous learning and improvement, and be willing to adjust your strategies as needed.

12. Practice self-care: Taking care of your physical, mental, and emotional well-being is crucial in navigating failure and building resilience. Practice self-care by getting enough sleep, eating healthily, engaging in regular exercise, and managing stress effectively. Prioritize self-care activities that bring you joy, relaxation, and rejuvenation. Taking care of yourself can help you stay mentally and emotionally strong to face challenges and overcome failure.

13. Cultivate a positive support system: Surround yourself with positive influences who can support and encourage you in your journey to overcome failure. Surround yourself with people who believe in your potential, offer constructive feedback, and provide encouragement. Avoid negative influences or toxic relationships that can bring you down or discourage you from pursuing your dreams. A positive support system can provide you with the motivation, inspiration, and perspective needed to navigate failure and keep moving forward.

14. Stay committed to your values and purpose: When facing failure, it's important to stay connected to your values and purpose. Reflect on what truly matters to you and what gives your life meaning and purpose. Stay committed to your core values and align your actions with your purpose. Having a sense of purpose can provide you with the motivation and resilience to overcome failure and continue pursuing your dreams with passion and determination.

Bouncing back from failure and continuing to pursue our dreams requires a combination of resilience, determination, self-belief, and adaptability. By acknowledging and processing emotions, reframing failure as an opportunity for growth, setting realistic goals, seeking support, practicing self-compassion, staying persistent, embracing innovation and creativity, and taking care of yourself, you can navigate failure in different areas of your life and use it as a stepping stone towards success. Remember that failure is a natural part of the learning process and can provide valuable insights and opportunities for growth. Stay committed to your dreams, stay resilient, and keep moving forward with courage and perseverance.

Overcoming Failure

Chapter 10: Thriving after Failure: Building a Resilient Future

Thrive after experiencing failure by building a resilient future.

Experiencing failure can be challenging, but it can also be an opportunity for growth and resilience. Thriving after failure involves learning from the experience, building a resilient mindset, and taking proactive steps towards a brighter future. Here are some ways to thrive after experiencing failure and build a resilient future:

1. Reflect and learn from the failure: Take time to reflect on the failure and identify the lessons learned. What went wrong? What could have been done differently? What did you learn about yourself, your strengths, and your weaknesses? Reflection and self-assessment can help you gain insights and wisdom from the failure, which can be applied to future endeavors.

2. Cultivate a growth mindset: Adopt a growth mindset, which is the belief that failure is an opportunity for learning and growth. Embrace challenges and setbacks as opportunities to improve, rather than as indicators of personal inadequacy. Reframe failure as a stepping stone towards success and view it as a chance to build resilience and develop new skills.

3. Set realistic goals and take action: Set realistic and achievable goals based on the lessons learned from the failure. Break down your goals into small, manageable steps and take action towards them. Setbacks may have dented your confidence, but taking proactive steps towards your goals can help you regain a sense of control and momentum.

4. Surround yourself with support: Build a support system of positive influences who can provide encouragement, advice, and support. Seek out mentors, friends, or family members who can offer guidance, perspective, and encouragement as you navigate through the aftermath of failure. Surrounding yourself with positive support can help you stay motivated and focused on your resilient future.

5. Practice self-compassion: Be kind and compassionate to yourself as you recover from failure. Avoid self-blame or harsh self-criticism, as it can hinder your ability to move forward. Treat yourself with the same kindness and understanding that you would offer to a friend facing similar challenges. Practice self-care, self-acceptance, and self-compassion to promote your emotional well-being and resilience.

6. Embrace innovation and creativity: Use the failure as an opportunity to tap into your creativity and innovation. Think outside the box and explore new approaches, strategies, or solutions. Embrace a mindset of curiosity, experimentation, and adaptability. Failure can sometimes open up new possibilities and avenues that you may not have considered before.

7. Build on your strengths: Recognize and leverage your strengths as you work towards building a resilient future. Identify your unique talents, skills, and qualities, and find ways to apply them to your goals and endeavors. Building on your strengths can boost your confidence, motivation, and resilience, and help you overcome challenges and setbacks.

8. Practice resilience: Cultivate resilience as you move forward from failure. Resilience is the ability to bounce back from setbacks, adapt to changes, and thrive in the face of adversity. Develop resilience by cultivating a positive mindset, maintaining a sense of purpose and meaning, fostering healthy coping strategies, and seeking support when needed. Resilience is a valuable skill that can help you navigate through challenging times and build a resilient future.

9. Stay committed to your vision: Stay committed to your vision and long-term goals, even after experiencing failure. Failure may be a setback, but it does not have to define your future. Stay focused on your vision, stay persistent in your efforts, and stay committed to your dreams. Remember that success often comes with setbacks along the way, and it's important to keep pushing forward with determination and perseverance.

Integrate the lessons learned from failure into our lives and use them as a foundation for future success.

Integrating the lessons learned from failure into our lives and using them as a foundation for future success involves reflection, introspection, and intentional action. Here are some steps to help you integrate the lessons learned from failure and use them to propel yourself towards future success:

1. Reflect on the lessons learned: Take time to reflect on the failure and the lessons you have learned from it. What went wrong? What could you have done differently? What were the key takeaways from the experience? Reflecting on the lessons learned allows you to gain valuable insights and wisdom from the failure.

2. Identify areas for improvement: Based on the lessons learned, identify specific areas for improvement. It could be your skills, knowledge, strategies, or mindset. Be honest with yourself and identify areas that need development or enhancement based on the lessons you have learned from the failure.

3. Set clear goals: Set clear and specific goals that are aligned with the lessons learned from the failure. Use the insights gained to set realistic and achievable goals that will help you move forward in a positive direction. Your goals should be specific, measurable, and time-bound to provide a clear roadmap for your future success.

4. Develop an action plan: Create an action plan that outlines the steps you need to take to achieve your goals. Break down your goals into smaller, manageable steps and create a timeline for each step. Having a clear action plan in place will help you stay focused and motivated as you work towards your future success.

5. Take intentional action: Take intentional action towards your goals, using the lessons learned as a guide. Be proactive and persistent in your efforts, and be willing to make adjustments along the way. Embrace a growth mindset and view challenges as opportunities for learning and improvement.

6. Embody resilience: Embody resilience as you move forward from failure. Embrace a mindset of perseverance, adaptability, and positivity. Expect setbacks along the way, but also recognize that you

have the capacity to overcome them. Stay committed to your goals and keep pushing forward despite challenges.

7. Cultivate self-compassion: Be kind and compassionate towards yourself as you integrate the lessons learned from failure into your life. Avoid self-blame or self-criticism, and instead practice self-compassion. Treat yourself with the same kindness and understanding that you would offer to a friend facing similar challenges.

8. Seek feedback and support: Seek feedback from mentors, coaches, or trusted individuals who can provide valuable insights and guidance. Surround yourself with a supportive network that can offer encouragement, motivation, and accountability. Having a support system in place can be instrumental in helping you integrate the lessons learned from failure into your life and achieving future success.

9. Stay open to learning: Remain open to continuous learning and growth. Recognize that failure is a part of the learning process and an opportunity for growth. Stay open to new perspectives, feedback, and insights. Embrace a mindset of continuous improvement and be willing to adjust your approach as needed based on the lessons learned.

10. Stay focused on your vision: Stay focused on your long-term vision and maintain a sense of purpose and motivation. Keep your eyes on the bigger picture and use the lessons learned from failure as a foundation to propel yourself towards your future success. Stay committed to your vision and stay persistent in your efforts.

Integrating the lessons learned from failure into our lives involves reflection, intentional action, resilience, self-compassion, and a growth mindset. By using the lessons learned as a guide, staying focused on our goals, and staying open to continuous learning, we can build a strong foundation for future success, even after experiencing failure.

Setting realistic goals

Setting realistic goals is an important aspect of achieving success, especially after experiencing failure. Realistic goals are those that are achievable, practical, and aligned with your current circumstances and resources. Here are some tips for setting realistic goals:

1. Reflect on your capabilities: Consider your current capabilities, resources, and limitations when setting your goals. Be realistic about what you can realistically achieve given your current situation. Assess your strengths, weaknesses, skills, knowledge, and available resources, and set goals that align with your abilities.

2. Consider your timeline: Set goals that are achievable within a reasonable timeframe. Consider your commitments, responsibilities, and other obligations in your life. Avoid setting overly aggressive or unrealistic timelines that may lead to disappointment or burnout. Be mindful of the time and effort required to achieve your goals.

3. Break down larger goals: If you have larger or long-term goals, break them down into smaller, manageable steps. This will make them more achievable and help you stay focused and motivated. Setting smaller milestones along the way allows you to track your progress and stay motivated as you work towards your larger goal.

4. Be specific and measurable: Set goals that are specific and measurable. Clearly define what you want to achieve and establish criteria to measure your progress. Specific and measurable goals allow you to track your progress and make adjustments as needed to stay on track.

5. Be flexible and adaptable: Be willing to adjust your goals as needed based on changing circumstances or new information. It's important to be flexible and adaptable as you work towards your goals, as unexpected challenges or opportunities may arise. Avoid being too rigid in your goal-setting process, and be open to making adjustments along the way.

6. Consider your motivation: Consider your motivation and commitment to the goals you are setting. Are you genuinely motivated to achieve these goals, or are they based on external pressures or expectations? Setting goals that align with your intrinsic motivation and personal values will increase your chances of success.

Overcoming Failure

7. Set challenging but achievable goals: While it's important to set realistic goals, also make sure they are challenging enough to push you outside of your comfort zone and inspire you to grow. Avoid setting goals that are too easy, as they may not provide enough motivation or satisfaction when achieved. Strike a balance between realistic and challenging goals that align with your abilities and aspirations.

8. Visualize success: Visualize yourself successfully achieving your goals. This can help you build confidence and motivation as you work towards your goals. Create a clear mental picture of yourself accomplishing your goals, and use it as a source of inspiration and motivation.

9. Get feedback and support: Seek feedback and support from trusted friends, mentors, or coaches. They can offer valuable insights, feedback, and guidance as you set and work towards your goals. Having a support system in place can also provide accountability and motivation.

10. Monitor and adjust: Regularly monitor your progress towards your goals and be willing to make adjustments as needed. If you find yourself struggling or off track, reevaluate your goals and make necessary adjustments to ensure they remain realistic and achievable.

Setting realistic goals is a key component of achieving success after experiencing failure. By considering your capabilities, timeline, motivation, and being adaptable, you can set goals that are achievable, motivating, and aligned with your aspirations. Regularly monitor your progress, seek support, and make adjustments as needed to stay on track towards achieving your goals.

Developing a growth mindset

Developing a growth mindset is the mindset that embraces challenges, sees failures as opportunities for learning and growth, believes in the potential for improvement, and fosters a positive attitude towards learning and personal development. Here are some practical tips for developing a growth mindset:

1. Embrace challenges: Embrace challenges as opportunities for growth rather than avoiding them. Challenges provide a chance to learn,

develop new skills, and expand your capabilities. Embracing challenges with a positive attitude can help you develop resilience and a growth-oriented mindset.

2. Reframe failure: View failure as a stepping stone to success rather than as a reflection of your worth or abilities. Reframe failure as a valuable learning experience that can provide insights, feedback, and opportunities for improvement. Embrace a mindset that sees failure as a natural part of the learning process.

3. Cultivate a positive attitude towards learning: Embrace a positive attitude towards learning, and recognize that learning is a lifelong process. Be open to new ideas, perspectives, and feedback. Embrace a curious and inquisitive mindset that seeks to learn and grow in all aspects of life.

4. Develop self-awareness: Develop self-awareness by reflecting on your strengths, weaknesses, beliefs, and attitudes towards learning and growth. Understand your thought patterns, emotions, and behaviors in response to challenges and failures. This self-awareness can help you identify areas for improvement and develop a more growth-oriented mindset.

5. Practice perseverance and resilience: Cultivate perseverance and resilience in the face of challenges and setbacks. Understand that progress may not always be linear, and setbacks are a natural part of the journey. Practice resilience by bouncing back from failures, setbacks, or disappointments, and staying committed to your goals and aspirations.

6. Adopt a "yet" mindset: Use the word "yet" in your vocabulary to embrace the idea of continuous improvement. For example, instead of saying "I can't do it," say "I can't do it yet." This shift in mindset recognizes that abilities can be developed over time with effort, practice, and perseverance.

7. Set learning goals: Set learning goals that are focused on personal growth and improvement rather than solely on achievement or external

validation. Embrace a mindset that values the process of learning and personal development, rather than just the outcome or end result.

8. Surround yourself with positive influences: Surround yourself with people who inspire and support your growth mindset. Seek out mentors, coaches, or peers who encourage a positive attitude towards learning, growth, and development. Avoid negative influences or individuals who discourage your growth mindset.

9. Emphasize effort and process over outcome: Focus on the effort you put into the learning process and the strategies you use to overcome challenges, rather than solely on the outcome or result. Recognize that the process of learning, growth, and development is more important than achieving immediate success.

10. Practice self-compassion: Be kind and compassionate towards yourself when facing challenges or setbacks. Treat yourself with the same kindness, understanding, and encouragement that you would offer to a friend. Embrace a mindset that allows for mistakes, imperfections, and setbacks, and uses them as opportunities for learning and growth.

Developing a growth mindset is a lifelong journey that requires intentional effort and practice. By embracing challenges, reframing failure, cultivating a positive attitude towards learning, developing self-awareness, practicing perseverance and resilience, adopting a "yet" mindset, setting learning goals, surrounding yourself with positive influences, emphasizing effort and process, and practicing self-compassion, you can foster a growth mindset that promotes personal growth, resilience, and success in various areas of your life.

Embracing a proactive approach to challenges.

Embracing a proactive approach to challenges involves taking ownership of the situation, actively seeking solutions, and taking steps towards overcoming the challenges rather than being passive or reactive. Here are some practical tips for embracing a proactive approach to challenges:

1. Take ownership: Acknowledge that challenges are a part of life, and take ownership of the situation by recognizing that you have the power to respond to challenges in a proactive manner. Avoid blaming external

factors or circumstances for the challenges you face, and instead focus on what you can control and influence.

2. Maintain a positive attitude: Adopt a positive attitude towards challenges, seeing them as opportunities for growth and learning. Embrace a mindset that views challenges as stepping stones towards personal development and improvement, rather than as insurmountable obstacles.

3. Seek solutions: Rather than dwelling on the problems or obstacles, focus on finding solutions. Take a proactive approach by actively seeking ways to overcome the challenges, and exploring different strategies or options for resolution. Be open to new ideas, perspectives, and feedback, and be willing to adapt and adjust your approach as needed.

4. Take action: Once you have identified potential solutions, take action towards implementing them. Break down the challenges into smaller, manageable steps, and take consistent action towards addressing them. Be proactive in initiating and implementing solutions, and avoid procrastination or inaction.

5. Be resourceful: Tap into your resources and strengths to tackle challenges. Utilize your skills, knowledge, experience, and support systems to come up with creative solutions. Seek help or guidance from others when needed, and be resourceful in finding ways to overcome the challenges.

6. Learn from setbacks: Embrace setbacks or failures as opportunities for learning and growth. Reflect on what worked and what didn't, and use the insights gained to adjust your approach and move forward in a more informed and proactive manner. Avoid dwelling on failures or setbacks, and use them as valuable feedback to improve your strategies and actions.

7. Stay resilient: Challenges may require resilience and perseverance to overcome. Embrace a resilient mindset by maintaining determination, perseverance, and a positive attitude, even when facing setbacks or

obstacles. Be willing to adapt, adjust, and learn from failures, and keep moving forward with a proactive and resilient mindset.

8. Foster a growth mindset: Cultivate a growth mindset, as discussed earlier, by embracing challenges as opportunities for learning and growth, and recognizing that abilities and skills can be developed over time with effort and practice. Foster a mindset that is open to learning, improvement, and personal development, and use challenges as a catalyst for growth.

9. Practice self-care: Taking care of your physical, mental, and emotional well-being is crucial in maintaining a proactive approach to challenges. Make sure to prioritize self-care, including getting enough rest, eating healthy, exercising, and managing stress. When you take care of yourself, you are better equipped to face challenges with a proactive mindset.

10. Stay persistent: Challenges may require time and effort to overcome, so it's important to stay persistent and committed to finding solutions. Avoid giving up or being discouraged by setbacks, and stay focused on taking proactive steps towards resolution. Keep a positive attitude, maintain your motivation, and stay persistent in your efforts.

Embracing a proactive approach to challenges involves taking ownership, maintaining a positive attitude, seeking solutions, taking action, being resourceful, learning from setbacks, staying resilient, fostering a growth mindset, practicing self-care, and staying persistent. By adopting a proactive mindset, you can effectively navigate challenges, overcome obstacles, and achieve success in various areas of your life.

Leverage our newfound resilience

Leveraging newfound resilience can be a powerful tool for personal growth and success. Resilience is the ability to bounce back, recover, and adapt in the face of challenges, setbacks, or adversity. When you develop resilience, you can effectively navigate difficult situations, overcome obstacles, and thrive in the face of adversity. Here are some ways to leverage newfound resilience:

1. Build on past successes: Reflect on previous experiences where you demonstrated resilience and overcame challenges. Consider the strategies, skills, and mindset that helped you overcome those challenges, and apply them to future situations. Draw on your past successes as a source of inspiration and motivation, and use them to fuel your confidence and belief in your ability to overcome new challenges.

2. Reframe challenges as opportunities: Develop a positive mindset towards challenges by reframing them as opportunities for growth, learning, and self-improvement. Embrace the idea that challenges are part of life's journey, and that they can provide valuable lessons, insights, and experiences that contribute to your personal development. View challenges as opportunities to strengthen your resilience and build your character.

3. Embrace adaptability: Resilience often involves adaptability - the ability to adjust, pivot, and find new ways of approaching a situation. Embrace a flexible mindset that allows you to adapt to changing circumstances, be open to new perspectives, and adjust your strategies as needed. Recognize that sometimes the path to success may require detours, and be willing to adapt and evolve along the way.

4. Set realistic goals: Set realistic and achievable goals that align with your values, strengths, and priorities. Break down larger goals into smaller, manageable steps, and celebrate your progress along the way. Setting realistic goals helps you stay focused, motivated, and resilient, as you can see tangible progress and stay committed to achieving them.

5. Practice self-compassion: Be kind and compassionate to yourself when facing challenges. Avoid harsh self-criticism or negative self-talk, and instead, practice self-compassion. Treat yourself with the same kindness, understanding, and support that you would offer to a friend facing similar challenges. Practice self-care, self-acceptance, and self-love, and give yourself the space and time needed to process emotions and recover from setbacks.

6. Cultivate a support system: Surround yourself with a supportive network of friends, family, mentors, or colleagues who can offer

Overcoming Failure

encouragement, guidance, and perspective during challenging times. Seek support when needed, and don't be afraid to ask for help. Having a support system can provide a valuable source of resilience, as you know that you are not alone in facing challenges and can rely on others for support.

7. Learn from setbacks: Embrace setbacks as opportunities for learning and growth. Reflect on what went wrong, what you could have done differently, and what you can learn from the experience. Use setbacks as feedback to improve your strategies, skills, and approaches in the future. Instead of dwelling on failures, use them as stepping stones towards future success.

8. Practice self-regulation: Emotions such as stress, frustration, or disappointment may arise when facing challenges. Practice self-regulation techniques, such as mindfulness, deep breathing, or other relaxation techniques, to manage your emotions and stay grounded. Avoid reacting impulsively or making hasty decisions based on emotions, and instead, take a step back, reflect, and respond thoughtfully and proactively.

9. Maintain a positive mindset: Cultivate a positive mindset that focuses on possibilities, strengths, and opportunities. Adopt an optimistic outlook towards challenges, and avoid dwelling on negativity or pessimism. Practice gratitude, positive self-talk, and visualization techniques to maintain a positive mindset, and reinforce your belief in your own resilience and ability to overcome challenges.

Confidence to pursue new opportunities, take calculated risks, and continue our journey towards personal and professional growth.

Confidence plays a critical role in pursuing new opportunities, taking calculated risks, and continuing our journey towards personal and professional growth. When we have confidence in ourselves and our abilities, we are more likely to embrace new challenges, push ourselves out of our comfort zones, and pursue opportunities that can lead to growth and success. Here are some ways to cultivate confidence:

1. Recognize and celebrate your strengths: Take the time to identify and acknowledge your strengths, skills, and accomplishments. Reflect on your past successes and achievements, and remind yourself of the unique qualities and abilities that you bring to the table. Celebrate your achievements, no matter how small they may seem, and use them as a foundation for building your confidence.

2. Set realistic and achievable goals: Set goals that are challenging yet attainable, and work towards achieving them. When you set realistic goals and make progress towards them, it boosts your confidence and motivation. Break down larger goals into smaller, manageable steps, and track your progress along the way. Celebrate your achievements and use them as evidence of your capabilities.

3. Learn from failure: Embrace failure as a learning opportunity rather than a reflection of your self-worth. When you encounter setbacks or failures, reflect on the lessons learned, and use them as stepping stones for growth. Avoid dwelling on self-doubt or negative self-talk, and instead, focus on the opportunities for improvement and learning from the experience.

4. Cultivate a growth mindset: Adopt a growth mindset, which is the belief that abilities and intelligence can be developed through effort, learning, and perseverance. Embrace challenges as opportunities for growth and learning, and view failures as temporary setbacks that can be overcome with effort and determination. Cultivate a positive attitude towards learning and improvement, and believe in your ability to develop new skills and abilities.

5. Take calculated risks: Taking risks is an essential part of personal and professional growth. However, it's important to take calculated risks, which involve evaluating the potential risks and benefits before making decisions. Assess the risks and benefits of a particular opportunity or challenge, weigh the pros and cons, and make informed decisions based on careful consideration. Taking calculated risks helps you build confidence in your ability to make wise decisions and navigate uncertainties.

6. Surround yourself with positive influences: Surround yourself with positive influences, such as supportive friends, mentors, or colleagues. Avoid negative influences or people who bring you down, and instead, seek out those who uplift and encourage you. Surrounding yourself with positive influences can boost your confidence and provide a supportive environment for personal and professional growth.

7. Continuously learn and develop new skills: Continuously invest in your personal and professional development by learning new skills, acquiring knowledge, and staying updated with industry trends. When you constantly improve yourself, it enhances your confidence and prepares you for new opportunities. Seek out learning opportunities, such as workshops, courses, or mentorships, and be proactive in acquiring new skills and knowledge.

8. Practice self-compassion: Be kind and compassionate towards yourself. Avoid self-criticism or negative self-talk, and instead, practice self-compassion. Treat yourself with the same kindness, understanding, and support that you would offer to a friend. Be patient with yourself as you navigate challenges and setbacks, and practice self-care to maintain a positive mindset and boost your confidence.

9. Visualize success: Use visualization techniques to imagine yourself succeeding in new opportunities or challenges. Visualize yourself confidently navigating challenges, achieving your goals, and embracing new opportunities. Visualization can help you build confidence by creating a positive mental image of your own success and reinforcing your belief in your abilities.

Overcoming Failure